PEACE TIME MARINES

PEACE TIME MARINES

WHIP RAWLINGS

PEACE TIME MARINES

This book is written to provide information and motivation to readers. Its purpose is not to render any type of psychological, legal, or professional advice of any kind. The content is the sole opinion and expression of the author, and not necessarily that of the publisher.

Copyright © 2020 by Whip Rawlings

All rights reserved. No part of this book may be reproduced, transmitted, or distributed in any form by any means, including, but not limited to, recording, photocopying, or taking screenshots of parts of the book, without prior written permission from the author or the publisher. Brief quotations for noncommercial purposes, such as book reviews, permitted by Fair Use of the U.S. Copyright Law, are allowed without written permissions, as long as such quotations do not cause damage to the book's commercial value. For permissions, write to the publisher, whose address is stated below.

Printed in the United States of America.

ISBN   978-1-64552-107-5   (Paperback)
ISBN   978-1-64552-108-2   (Digital)

Lettra Press books may be ordered through booksellers or by contacting:

Lettra Press LLC
30 N Gould St. Suite 4753
Sheridan, WY 82801, USA
1 303-586-1431 | info@lettrapress.com
www.lettrapress.com

INTRODUCTION

It was brought to my attention, a great number of civilians believe, unless you were fighting in a war zone, your not as great a patriot as those that did fight in a war. Unfortunately, this attitude carries over to the deparment of defense. The Marines I served with, including myself, suffered injuries seen and unseen during training. Any large Corporation in America would compensate their employees for injuries on the job. My question is, "why is the U.S. government the exception to the rule?" Some injuries are mental and other unjuries are physical. In either case the government has deind veteran claims by the hundred thousands. In my case, injuries related to Desert storm and arthritis caused by sleeping on ice for twelve weeks in South Korea, including training in sweltering 120 degrees heat in 29 Palms California. During those trainings I suffered 50% hearing loss in my left ear while shooting artillery cannon's for eight years. Carring 100 lbs artillery shells and riding in the back of a five ton truck with artillery shells bouncing in the air, land on top of my legs.

During the time I prep for Desert Storm, my unit was taken to camp atteberry for our final medical treatment. The treatment included a series of injections and pills. Months later I found myself gravely ill from the affects of the medication, including a PD pill, a drug that was suppose to counter the effects of chemical agents. My bones ached, rash covered my chest, shoulders, forehead and caused massive memory loss. I had headaches for six months at a time, I was totally exhausted for months and my muscles ached from head to toe. This course ran its cycle over and over, six months at a time. I went to the VA hospital for a full chem panel, but the medical findings were inconclusive.

Not a shot was fired at the enemy during that time, but never the less I was a silent casualty of war. It took ten years before I become eligible to be listed as service connect with the military, therefore; I lived with the pain for years, paying for my health care out of pocket, for something the civilian doctors didn't have a clue how to treat. Even though I had medical proof, documenting my Gulf war symptoms over a course of ten years, the military shoved my file deep in the crevices of the records room, until a diligent rep from one of the contracting departments discovered the file and filed for a hearing. Like myself, other military personel suffer the same injustice, with little hope of ever receiving financial compensation or medical treatment.

I am a proud patriot, Peace Time Marines.

I woke up to another warm spring morning, one day closer to transitioning out of childhood into adulthood and it scared me into a new reality. The reality of pay my own bills, keeping a roof over my head. I felt the course of my life was changing. I could know longer stay with them my comfort zone and continue to live within the comforts of my daily routine.

Graduation from high school was within reach and in a months time I would be socially promoted into the civilian world of employment. It didn't matter that I had marginal grades, the education system was in continuous motion and was not going to stop or slow down for a student who was not academically up to standards. I would have to leave the nest, expand my wings and soar like an Eagle or fall from heaven like Michael the angelic angel. My lifes predestination was set in place like the stones on a building and would not change until I recognized a change needed to be made.

I was nervous but excited, I could smell my emancipation floating in the air. I was mentally exhausted thinking about paying my own rent, utility bills, car payment and other life changing anomalies adults did to create life after adolescents. I was scared out of my mind at the possibility of failing the ASVB exam for the second time. I knew I had to change my methods of study if joining the marines was going to become a reality, so I acquired four pages of word knowledge. The words covered front and back of the page.

I sat in my room for three days not participating in extra curriculum activities at the basketball court or hanging out with girl. I buckled down in my room with my face to the grind stone until I knew the list back and forth. In between study times I would stand in the mirror and imagine myself wearing a set of dress blues. The white hat with a black brim, flank by gold buttons on each sides, placed squarely on my head. The high collar with two gold Marine Corps emblems. The mirror turn foggy then cleared, all the sudden my chin was squared and I was a Marine.

My only focal point at that time was becoming a United States Marine, nothing else mattered, not even getting my high school diploma or the fact that I was leaving my hometown and people that I loved behind. However; I was missing a very important part of the puzzle. I didn't know what I was getting into. I didn't know about the $20,000 recruiting bonus or the difference between open and closed contract. I just wanted to be challenged. I wanted to see if I could stand on my own 2 feet and take whatever pressure they could dish out. My rude awaking would soon be played out in 16 weeks of hell.

Going up without a father created a huge gap of uncertainty in my mind. I question everything I did, right down to the smallest detail. I was never sure if I was making the right decision about anything. I wasn't taught to think outside of the small community where I lived, I didn't think about other cultures or the way they lived. Everything I learned, I learn from the streets and the people I associated with leaving me miss informed and a huge gap in cultural understanding. However, my mother did teach me how to respect others and things that belong to other people.

My mother never overly indulge me, I received the basic needs, shoes, clothing, food, and roof over my head, everything outside the rim of my basic needs I had to make do for myself. Learning how to become a man with a single parent had a different flavor than young boys that had two live in parents. I had to learn from the empty uniforms in the small radius within my enclave. Most of the young fathers worked in plants of some type or factories or as general labors. I don't recall any African American white collar workers living in my neighborhood.

All the men in my life spent their time chasing women, if they weren't chasing women they were getting drunk at a local bar on Indiana Avenue, or planning some scheme to get some sort of ill- gotten gains. I never saw an example of a black man going to college, medical or law school. I never knew what was career or educationally possible, other than being a janitor, sport figure, or general labor.

The closest I came to seeing an example of a man working at a steady job was my stepfather. He would get up at four in the morning, go to work, then come home sloppy drunk at 10 PM. He found his place at the kitchen table after removing his dinner from the stove. His daily routine was as precise as the count down before NASA launched a ship into space.

He quietly and drunkenly walked into the house never uttering a word he'd remove his plate that was warming in the oven, slumped down in his chair, eat his gravy covered pork chops with mash potatoes, then stagger upstairs. He slowly staggered by, brushing against me, not saying a word. He made his way up to the top of the staircase landing, turned into his bedroom then flopped down on the bed and passed out. He was the most direct example in my life that I had of what a man did on a daily basis. I didn't know any better because I didn't have any better examples.

I did have an uncle named George who worked at Regen's bakery, and I'm pretty sure he went to work everyday on time for 30 years. He and his wife Dorothy, my mothers sister always had the newest cars in the family. They had a small dainty two bedroom house with plastic covering the couch and chairs. I found it odd that my auntie was a school teacher yet her husband couldn't read a word, but he was good with his hands and could build almost anything as well as being an excellent mechanic. I do believe he would've been a good role model but I only saw him once every five or six months when he came by the house with a box of stale donuts trying to put a smile on our face, but I was no longer a little kid I was 18 years old and a box of stale glazed donuts wasn't going to change the dynamics of my life in the next two months.

My life was changing for sure, I was growing as a person and the path that I had chosen I must travel alone. Later that day I made my way to the A-fee station were more than 50 other individuals of different ethical backgrounds and genders were all taking the same test but for different branches of the service. I was very proud to be one of the few in the room that was taking the Marine Corps exam but in hindsight I was one of the few idiots that was taking the Marine Corps exam. I finish the exam and was escorted into the other room, anyone that failed the exam was shown the door and was told not to return for six months.

I was so excited I couldn't hold it inside, I told everyone, even the people on the bus, I ran down 29th and Talbott as though I won the lottery. Once I approached my front door I stopped, compose myself and walked in the house as cool as a glass of water in the summer time. I set at the kitchen table, crossed my legs and grabbed a section of the Indianapolis Star. My mother stared at me as she stirred her folgers coffee.

"Where have you been all day?" She ask.

"I was at the recruiting station, I took the Marine Corps exam and passed it, my departure date is July 18." I said.

My mothers eyes got big and suddenly she stop sipping her coffee and began haranguing me about the corp.

"Why in the hell did you join the Marines? Are you crazy?"

"I want to be tested, I want to know who I am and if I can stand on my own two feet, this is something that I must do alone".

"I hope you know what the hell you're doing". She said. "Well, if I don't we're going to find out July 18".

Later that evening I setting my room wondering if I had made the mistake. Visions of the old Marine Corps movies, ravitched my every waking thought. I couldn't sleep a wink, I swear I must had been awoke for five days straight. A month and a half later I was being picked up by my Marine recruiter at 9 AM in the morning to be transported to the recruiting station for final processing and a flight to San Diego California. My mother and I stood outside that morning waiting for the recruiter to arrive, as usual he pulled up in a little ford escort with the Marine Corps emblem on the side.

I began dragging the seabag toward the car, the recruiter stepped out of the car. "Where are you going with that"? "He said.

"To boot camp" I said

'Recruiter' "You don't need that, I just need you".

So I gave the bag back to my mother and hopped in the front seat of the recruiters car. As the car drove away my mother stood in the front yard watching me drive off, she knew I had signed up to take a shot trip through hell but there was nothing she can do. With teary-eyes and a slight lump in her throat, she managed to summons enough strength to wave a final goodbye. I stared at her out the window until the car turn the corner on 30th Street, I barely caught a glimpse of her struggling to drag the sea bag back up the steps into the house.

I scanned the neighborhood with my eyes hoping to catch a glimpse of someone I knew so I could wave goodbye to them but no one was around. It was as if the streets were purposely empty, no one saw me leave, there was no one to say good luck or I'll see you when you get back, it made me feel empty, unloved and alone. For the first time in my life 29th and Talbott was empty, there wasn't a soul to be found, everyone had disappeared into their own lives and I was on my way to make a profound statement or come back a baby blue Marine. Baby blue Marines are the individuals the failed boot camp. They were dressed up in white T-shirts, a blue baseball hat and a blue scarf around their neck, then escorted to the front gate. I was determined not to be a big blue Marine. This was the moment I self actualized in my dreams, the moment that would make or break my spirit forever.

There were a lot of first for me that day, first time I've flown on the plane, the first time I would visit California, the first time I would feel what it was like to miss my mother and the first time I would miss someone that I cared deeply about.

The most significant thing of all, I was leaving as Mikey but I will return a Marine. My plane lifted off with trusters in full gear settling above the majasted clouds. In my mind I waved goodbye to Indianapolis and thanking the city for my childhood memories, the late summer nights and the cold winter morning.

After six hours of flying the 747 dipped its wings making a pivital turn directly over Marine Corp Recurite Depot. Exercise equipment stretched across a half mile long dusty barren field. Barrackes were lined up perfectly in a row as far as the eye could see.

WHERE IT ALL BEGAN

We touched down in San Diego at 7 PM that evening. The Marine Corps recruit Depot bus was parked right outside terminal. All Marine recruits boarded the bus and waiting for headcount before heading towards the base. I feel reassured uncomfortable, comfortable enough to pop a piece of gum in my mouth. I set back and watch the civilian women on the street wearing bikinis and the magnificent display of palm trees from one endless block to the other. I've never seen anythin like it. The sky was much different then the sky in Indianapolis. The sky appear to be wider, more open and ages younger then the sky that nestled above Indianapolis.

The bus pool directly up to the gate, a Marine standing has post waved us through. The bus stopped in a dimly lit parking lot. Rolls of yellow footprints we are visiting from the window. I sat back popping my gum, I couldn't help but wonder why would someone paint all of those footprints on ground. Seconds later the bus tilted to one side. A 230 pound well-built drill instructor stepped onto the bus.

"Shut the fuck up!" He yelled.

"You got 39 seconds to get your ass off at his bus and 29 of them are up, Move!" He yelled with a thunderous voice.

All the young recruits began scrambling for their lives, every man for himself, no one want to be the last person off the bus. And within seconds my questions about the yellow footprints were answered.

We scrambled our way to lining up on the footprints. 15 Drill instructors came out of nowhere yelling and screaming. It was as if they appeared right out of the ground pushed out of hell by Satan himself. It Was the most intense moment I had experience to this date in my life. Drill instructors on each side pressing their campaign hats into the side of my head, yelling in my ears commands I couldn't understand.

We ran in place for what seemed like an hour until one marine recruit collapsed lifelessly to the ground. I thought he was dead but I had no time to be a hero I had to save my own ass. So I lift my knees high in the air hitting my chest, while the drill instructors yelled, spitting in my face almost knocking me over with their campaign had press firmly to the side of my head. I never heard so much profanity in my life. It was as if it was a new form of language a vernacular I never heard before. I was called bitch five times before I got my first haircut.

The night was dangerously crazy, everything was moving at an exaggerated fast pace. We got our heads shaved, stripped naked, issued new clothing and inventoried all our personal clothing then March the cross grinder to receiving barracks. Through all the chaos I managed to watch the firey red sun disappear behind the red roof tops lining the edges of MCRD.

All 80 of stripped down to our bare essentials and shovel to the shower 40 recruits at a time. I never seen another male genitalia before and it wasn't a pleasant expanse. I knew this would be a long 82 training days.

We were in bed by 1 AM. I was thoroughly shaken up, I didn't know what just happened or if I could keep up with this fanatic pace for long. Our misfortune was the receiving barracks were located right next to the San Diego airport, I could see the planes landed and take off behind the 12 foot high wooden fence. The airplanes seemed so close it was as if I could reach out of my window and touch their wings. Freedom was just on the other side of the fence and the more they precious the more temptation was setting in.

Glover the kid I flew from Indianapolis to San Diego with wanted to go (UA) meaning unauthorized absence. We decided once everyone was sleep we were going to jumped the fence and crawl into the landing gear of the airplane. I close my eyes for a brief second waiting for everyone around me to go to sleep, before I knew it, it was 4 AM, the lights flickered on and trash cans were being thrown about the squad bay.

Drill instructors running, screaming and yelling, getting in our faces and before we could thing straight and wiped the morning dew for my eyes we were walking down the street in a big mob, flashlights in our hands, our knowledge and toothpaste in our cargo pockets, our shirts button all the way to the top. Drill instructors yelling at the top of their lungs, calling cadence in an untraditional fashion as we try to get in step while marching down the streets toward the chow hall.

I was starving and confused, it was dark and cold, I could barley see 3 feet in front of me, we were rushed through the chow hall like cows, given two minutes to swallow what ever food we can get in us, then pushed out the back door and forest marched back to the barracks at an insane pace. We scrubbed and cleaned the showers and bathroom floors with tooth brushes. Everything was at an extremely fast pace with the exception of getting out of receiving barracks or being picked up by our new drill instructors. It has been two weeks and we were still hanging around the receiving barracks waiting for our 82 training days to begin. We practice cleaning the barracks and freeing our uniforms of (iris pendants) threads hanging from our uniforms.

Then all of a sudden there were three drill instructors kicking our sea bags down the steps, tossing our uniforms and boots over the railing of the balcony. Everyone got treated the same because we all look the same in the eyes of the drill instructors, we were all equal idiots. The torture continued on for 20 minutes as we walked to our new barracks. 20 minutes that seemingly took an hour before we where able to reached the barracks. The drill instructors couldn't resist playing head games, kicking our cover blocks ahead of us as we walked in a disorganized fashion. Walking one right on top of the other, asshole to belly button! They yelled, screaming and spiting in our faces while we locked eyes straight forward on the back of the head of the man in front of us.

The pace was excruciatingly fast, I was beginning to feel the effects of hunger from the corner piece of bread and one spoon of eggs I was able to shove in my mouth before we were dragged from the chow hall and tossed in a half-baked formation. Rush rush rush rush and before I knew it night had fallen upon us. Every waking minute was occupied by what they wanted us to think, see, hear and do. By 9 o'clock pm we were all in bed laying at attention on the top of our Olive drab wool blankets listening to the bugle play taps. I try to stay awake by listening to the comforting sound of the crickets but there were none, all I could here was the planes taking off carrying my freedom with it and landing with the new batch of recruit sucker bait at the airport next door. I may as well be dead I thought, I was just in the first week a Boot camp and the end of 82 training days was more than three months away. It pained me to think about it, I just wanted out the fastest way I could get out. But the Marines had my name on contract and I we belong to them for the next four years.

These were 82 of the most intense days of my life but I was made the better man for it. During those 82 days Cindy and I touch bases once again and I have to say her letters did help get me through boot camp. Cindy couldn't help expressing the way she felt about me, she planet kisses on the envelope of every letter. Each time I got a letter with the imprint of lips, the smell of perfume, or salutations written on the outside of the envelope, I got thrashed by my drill instructors. I was removed from squaw bay and made to roll around in the dirt and perform mountain climbers, side straddle hops and bend and thrust for every salutation or lip imprint on the outside of the envelope. I tried my best to tell her don't write or put anything on the outside of the envelope but she never listen and I paid dearly for her affectionate salutations.

I became friends with a young marine name Sampson. I thought it was really cool that he was from Chicago and I was from the neighboring city next-door. One day the drill instructors had the bright idea of placing Sampson in charge of the rifle rack, wear more then 80 M16 rifles were locked away. He was also given the responsibility of being the platoon guide on Baron, until one day he lost the keys to the rifle rack. The drill instructors became infuriated and thrash Sampson up-and-down the squad bay, doing push-ups, setups and mountain climbers until he sweat out a pool of blood. The drill instructor then grabbed Sampson's foot locker and tossed it against the wall, out came the keys sliding down the squad bay stopping at the front of my feet as I stood at attention watching the incident unfold.

Sampson was pulled into the drill instructors office, they slammed him against the wall lockers and bulkhead then tossed him out into the squad bay where he landed on his face sliding almost through the double exit doors. I was glad he was okay, I smiled and chuckled to myself as he ran back and stood at attention in front of his rack. His goofy act provided me with great comic relief at a time I was stressed to the point of breaking.

Every morning was the same for the next 82 days, fast-paced, pushing, shoving and yelling. Each day started with a shit, shower and shave. We played mind games, ripping our beds apart and putting them back together as fast as we could. This was our usual 4:30 AM ritual before we went to breakfast. We were marched to breakfast as though we were running the 50 yard dash. We were new to the corp and not yet discipline.

Everything we did we did together in close proximity of one another. They called it asshole to belly button. Even in the chow line we were not allowed to look anywhere other than the man's head in front of us. Once we reach the serving line we locked eyes on the wall in front of us and sidestep our way through the chow line. I locked eyes with an authoritative looking Major. Because I had a good nature and wasn't fully aware of Marine Corps policy, as a kind gesture I smiled at the Major.

The major pounced on me like a lion on a hyena, right up to me ass-hole to belly button style, and pressed his nose against mines.

"Do you want to go to jail"? He asked in a very convincing Voice, "Sir, no sir" I said, with a nervous expression.

"Then wiped that fucking smile off your face".

My drill instructor stood at the back of the chow hall observing what had just taken place. I could feel the telepathic waves of anger reflecting off the side of my face as my drill instructor ran towards me seemingly at 100 miles an hour then pressing his campaign cover to the side of my head. The pressure was so great I was slightly knocked off balance as he leaned over and whispered in my ear.

"You fucking owe me bitch."

I was so traumatized I could barely eat my breakfast with the thought of going to jail or being thrashed by my drill instructor, either way it wouldn't have to pay the wages of my boot camp sins.

Right after we had our limited portions of food we returned to the barracks and change into our PT gear then headed to the obstacle course for a 3 mile run alongside the wooden fence line separating the Marine Corps base from the airport. I couldn't help but be envious every time I saw the naval sailors standing outside smoking a cigarette and laughing at us while we ran 3 miles in 100° weather.

The Navy boot camp was located next door to MCRD, there was one small difference, they were on a six week vacation and we were going through 16 weeks of hell. The naval Boot Camp program was very different, they ate chow whenever they wanted too and wasn't forced to eat vegetables like I was. My drill instructor would stand behind me in the chow line at breakfast, lunch and dinner time and order the line personnel to put stacks of Broccoli, collie flower, and carrots on my plate. I would take the vegetables and give them to the Marine next to me or hide them in my ice cream cup and cover the vegetables with napkins.

Sometimes my drill instructor would stand by the exit and inspect my tray, if I still had vegetables on my plate he would stand over me until I ate them but most of the time I was able to get away with throwing them in the trash. The drill instructor said I would need the vegetables to get up Mount motherfucker. I didn't understand what he meant at the time because it was too early in my training, and I was still adjusting to all the yelling and screaming at 4 AM.

The sailors stood outside on their balcony's smoking cigarettes, laughing, pointing at us as we ran along the fence line in the sweltering heat. Sampson and I were running neck to neck and all of a sudden he disappear, someone shoved him into a fire hydrant breaking his right leg. I finished my run around 21 minutes, then down the strip came Sampson, he completed the 3 mile run in 24 minutes with a broken leg. The drill instructor didn't seem to care that Sampson had just broken his leg, he ordered Sampson to continue running until he reached the ambulance, so Sampson limped his way over to the ambulance, and disappeared for three days.

The drill instructors could have dropped him from the platoon at this point but he demonstrated courage and heart when he finished the 3 mile run in 24 minutes with a broken leg. Having a broken leg aided Sampson with skating from a lot of duties. He didn't have to March to church, he was allowed to stay in the barracks and watch all the gear. Everyone went to church, it didn't matter what religion you were, you was forced to attend. After church we spent Sunday afternoon washing our clothes on a concrete slab then hanging our clothes up on a clothes line. We finish the weekend off with polishing our boots and reading our knowledge while the drill instructor paced up and down the squad bay.13

After the second month my sleep had a new definition, the definition of military time. I no longer slept until eight in the morning, my mind was now preset to 4 AM. We packed our gear and lined up in formation on the parade grinder, we were on our way to Camp Pendleton for marksmanship training. I was feeling pretty cocky at this point I even felt like I could complete the entire 16 weeks of training. We were allowed to unbutton our collars, roll up our sleeves and blouse our trousers. I had a smile hidden inside that I dare not reveal in front of my drill instructors, but I must admit I was feeling pretty good, so good that I leaned over and spit on the parade deck.

The drill instructor saw me out of the corner of his eye. He yelled. "get your ass over here private" I ran over to the drill instructor and lock my body at attention, he leaned forward pressing his campaign hat against my forehead, he said," lick it up!" He stare deep into my eyes as I took a deep breath I squatted down and wiped the spit up with my right hand. I locked my body at attention assuming the worst. I thought for sure I was going to jail, but he gave me a stern look and said, "Get on the bus, crazy one".

The bus ride from San Diego to Camp Pendleton Took about 45 minutes. We sat at attention the whole time locking our eyes on the back of the head of the man in front of us. My drill instructor set at the front of the bus and begin to doze off. I took the opportunity to enjoy the scenic view, I relax my shoulders and shifted my eyes out side of the window getting a QuickView of the red roof tops that we stared at from our barracks for the last two months. It looked just like the pictures in the right on magazine, beaches stretching along the coast of the highways and palm trees as far as the eye could see.

My day dreaming came to an abrupt end once the bus came to a screeching stop, all hell broke loose once again. The harassment continued even while we set on bleachers in the marksmanship class. Our drill instructor would tap 10 of us on the shoulder then take us behind the bleachers and thrash us for 15 minutes, making us roll around in the sand until our bodies was totally covered from head to toe, "Make it rain" he yelled as we threw sand in the air.

Once we were filthy from head to toe he would get 10 fresh recruits until he went through the entire platoon. I couldn't focus or learned a dame thing, every time they try to teach us something the drill instructor fines a way to harass us in the midst of our military education. I was qualifying at the marksman skill level, but I was losing confidence fast. A young recruit next to me have been recycle back two weeks because he failed marksmanship training. I wasn't about to repeat any cycle, so I pretended as though I couldn't see the target and needed glasses. I was pulled from the firing line and told to guard all the file cabinets and sea bags on the parade grinder. The shooting finally stopped as the young recruits completed marksmanship qualification, everyone lined up to turn in their empty shell casing and wooden ammo blocks. All the sudden there was a Single shot fired and within seconds one of the drill instructors came running towards me asking for a file on the Private that shot himself, then ran back to administer first aid.

The young marine recruit that stood next to me killed himself rather than repeat another two weeks of hell. We returned to San Diego for our last month of boot camp, part of our training included working in the chow hall or working in the lawn maintenance. Two weeks after that we packed up once again to return to camp pendleton for infantry training school. We were still at an incredible pace and that pace would intensify once we went through the infiltration course with machine guns firing over our heads as we crawled on our stomachs under Bob-wire, trying not to trip the wires setting off the night flairs. I thought it was easy and fun but other recruits thought it was a horrible ordeal to go through. We slept outside the infiltration course that night and awoke to a mountain towering 10 miles up into the air.

We wore full combat gear including a back pack, helmet and a long wooden shovel that beat the crap out of our leg as we climb steadily up the mountain at an insanely fast-paced. My drill instructor was right, I did need the vegetables and I was paying the price for dumping them in the trash. The mountain was steep, so steep that my face nearly scraped the ground as I went up, I watched the first platoon flag as it turned the corner and disappear, I thought for sure we were at the top but as I turn the corner the flag was still going up and up. I had no thoughts of home in my head, I didn't even think about finger banging Cindy threw her pretty pink panties.

I was in excruciating pain from head to toe, the Marine that I gave my vegetables too asked if I wanted to grab onto his backpack, but I was too proud, so I sucked it up and picked a focal point and up the mountain I went. As soon as we got to the top of the mountain our drill instructors began to bin and thrust us.

"Make it rain!"

They yelled as we rolled around in the dirt. The dirt cling to our bodies because our camouflage utilities were saturated with sweat. Our face was covered with dirt and sweat slowly turning into mud with small thorns from the brush lying on the ground sticking out of our trousers. We stood at attention with our eyes locked on the back of the head of the man in front of us. We couldn't blink, speak or wipe the sweat and mud for our face.

All I could think about was the short three weeks I had left and I be done with this nightmare. We return to MCRD, Marine Corp Recruit Depot two weeks after arriving at infantry training school. All we had left was guard duty then we turned our rifles in and prepare for graduation. The Marine Corps boot camp definitely change me, my good nature have been soured and my infectious smile had all but disappeared.

I had been beaten on and beaten up for 82 training days in a life I wouldn't recommend for my children or grandchildren, in fact I would recommend it for anyone. Three weeks later I was back in Indianapolis a different man with different perspectives but one agenda, after two weeks of leave I was on my way to Camp Pendleton where my tour of duty would begin. Our routine wasn't much different from boot camp, the only difference was I didn't have drill instructors yelling in my face and the pace was slightly slower, other than that it was still the suck. Cindy and I wrote each other everyday, I'd go home to visit twice a year accept for the spring of 1979. I was still just a 19-year-old kid running around the barracks pulling pranks on the older Marines. I always believed it's not where you live but how you live.

Living in marine barracks was very boring at times especially if you didn't have money. I spend most my time at the recreation center on base playing pool or watching one of the two TV stations. Sometimes I became very mischievous, one Sunday I had absolutely nothing to do, so I began organizing my room, I was cleaning out an old wall locker. While shuffling through the wall lockers I found a mask of a scary monster stuffed away at the bottom of the empty locker. I put the mask on and walked around the barracks knocking on doors, unexpectedly scaring everyone that opened the door. The biggest, toughest guys in unit would slam the door in my face, until they realize it was just a mask. I went from door-to-door scaring everyone I could until it was my time to return to duty desk.

It was my turn to stand duty that night but I wasn't sleepy so I sat outside on the steps of the barracks and listen to the quietness of the night. I often thought about Cindy, how much I missed her. I enviously watch the city buses leave the base loaded down with Marines trying to escape for the weekend in Oceanside. Later that evening I was summonsed to put on my cartridge belt and sit at the NCO desk, occasionally I would patrolled the hallways of the barracks ensuring that no rooms are broken into and there were no fights. Anything that happened out of the ordinary I'd record it in my duty log and call the duty NCO or Officer of the day.

Having duty on the weekends was a much dislike responsibility each Marine perform monthly. Most of the Marines would offered to pay someone $30 to stand their Post on the weekend. I obliged them as long as they paid me $30 cash upfront. I wasn't familiar with Oceanside nor the people that inhabit the city, so I spend most of my time hanging out on the base and I thought to myself "since I'm going to be here anyway I may as well get paid for it. So I sat at the duty NCO desk reading my magazines and counting my new found wealth.

One night while patrolling the barracks I began to smell smoke, I alerted the duty NCO and showed him the location of the fire, we bang on the door trying to wake the sleeping Marine, but to no avail. I was ordered by the duty NCO to climb through the window and open the door, I did as I was ordered. I climbed through the window and discovered a Marine sleeping on a burning mattress, I open the door, then went back and grab the Marine under the arm pits and drag him in the hallway to safety, then dousing the mattress with several buckets of water.

The next week I was hurled as a hero and given a meritorious mast certificate, nothing change for me at that point I was still an E-3 and performing every shit detail the other seasoned Marines didn't want to do. If the Canon base plates need to be grease, I was sent up the hill to the gun park to grease all six bass plates for the cannons. No liberty was granted until all the rust was removed from all six cannons and the base plates were greased for the weekend. So I ran up the hill in the rain slipping and sliding in the mud as I dug the toe of my boots into the mud, the Marines stood down the hill sarcastically cheering me on.

"Hurry up you boot!" "come on get a move on boot"!

Boot was a derogatory term used for Marines fresh out of boot camp, and I was as green as they came. So I climbed the hill and greased all six cannons base plates then I ran back down the hill demonstrating sure footed accuracy as if I was a goat scaling the Rocky Mountains, back down through the brush cover trench and up the slight incline to the paved parking lot where formation was being held.

My unit was still chanting. "Boot boot boot boot!

I stood in formation soaking wet listening to the chants, my highly spit shined boots were cover with a clay like mud, my camouflage utilities were soaked from head to toe. It was pouring down rain at this point, we stood at attention silently looking and listening to the first sergeant pontificated the rules of how we should conduct ourselves while on weekend liberty and finally he yelled.

"Dismissed!"

I ran from the formation back to the barracks and began stripping my uniform off as my foot hit the door. I quickly through my clothes in the washer and jumped in the shower to wash off the grease deep in the pores of my skin.

I could see a person's head poking back and forth on the other side of the shower wall and occasionally peeking around the corner into the shower, I paid no attention because there were no females on base. Soon I discovered it was Peterson, the units homosexual who had been beaten up more than once for his unsolicited sexual comment. Peterson was very brash and would walk right up to you and tell you how I felt. Several weeks later Peterson made sexual innuendo's to the wrong marine at the wrong time, resulting with him being beaten half to death. Once Peterson was released from the hospital, he was given an other than honorable discharge.

Take a shower after Boot Camp was slightly different, we continue to shower in open squad bay but we could decide what time do you want to take a shower. I showered early mornings or late in the evening normally having the shower all to myself, I wrapped my towel around my waist, I slipped and slid my way back to my room, my shower shoes sticking to the floor eventually breaking apart leaving one shower shoe in the hallway as I hobble back to my room on one leg.

I was starving, the aroma coming from the chow hall was fiercely wetting my appetite, I quickly got dressed in my civilian clothes, pausing for a brief second to stare out the window at the line of Marines that stretched around the chow hall. Marines stood in the pouring rain waiting to enter the building. I was very fortunate I could sit in the warmth of my room and watch the line shrink. It was an off payday, everyone was broke, this was very typical for young Marines. If you were an E-1 to E-3 you only got paid $600.00 a month. Half our money was spent on the roach coach, a lunch wagon that came around the barrack's blowing its horn at night soliciting snacks and getting Marines to spend the last bit of their pay. The other half of our money was spend at bars in town, movies, and on women at the possibility of having a one night stand. I wasn't broke, I was one of the few young Marines in the camp that had money. I have a pocket full of money and no where to go.

I spend most of my time at the base gym, hitting the punching bag, jump roping or just reading a book in my room. I wasn't familiar with my new surroundings, therefore; I only want to town when I was with a group of trusted friends. Most of the guys I hung around with were young and inexperience like myself. We didn't hang out in bars as the mature guys did. Sampson and I would go to the beach, the mall, movies, or to Burger King.

He hobbled along beside me, casket on his leg and all. I wasn't a party type of guy, but if I wanted too, I can go in a bar and drink even though I was underage. The bar keeper didn't care about age he only care about how much money they could get us to spend. Every night was the same once we left town, everyone would crowd around the bus stop in front of Hogies corner and rushed the door before the bus would door open or come to a complete stop. The bus driver would just take off and go to the next bus stop making us chase the bus to the next block. Sampson it was short of money.

I don't know how he did it but he managed to spend all but $.20 of his bus money. So we concocted a plan. I gave Samson 10 pennies and told him as soon as I put my bus money in he should put his bus money in on top of mines. This scam worked.

Once we got on the bus there was standing room only. When the bus enter the gate to the base the military police (MP'S) made everyone get off the bus, and conducted an informal search of the bus and all the Marines riding on it.

Within 20 minutes we were back on our way. The Marines thought the bus was moving too slow so we rock the bus back-and-forth demanding that the bus driver go faster. The driver pulled to the side of the road and demanded that we stop rocking the bus. The more he demanded the more we rock the bus almost turning it on its side. The bus driver became so scared he jumped in his driver's seat and race down los pocus road breaking the speed limit by at least 15 miles per hour. Every night it was the same thing, and every night I just sat back in my seat and laugh. We worked hard and we played hard as well.

Most of my free time I spent in the barracks writing letters to Cindy and thinking about my old friends in my neighborhood. What were they doing and who was at the basketball court? I thought about my mom and how I've missed living in her house, I thought about my oldest brother and his sexual escapades. I thought about my brother Denton in the army and my sister Sherry in the Air Force. I thought about how nice it would've been if I had stayed home and got a regular job and had a regular life. But that was no longer my life, the corp was my new reality. Something inside of me was changing but I didn't know what it was. Maybe I was becoming a man, or maybe I was becoming a professional killer, whatever it was changing inside of me would alter my thought process forever. I loved the beach and the palm trees and the entire California atmosphere, it was far different from Indiana.

California seemed very fast paced, women would roller skate along the beach wearing bikinis. You would've never saw anything like that Indiana, she would have been arrested and put in jail for indecent exposure. California even have nude beaches that I spend most of my time trying to find but never succeeded. I was told they were 45 minutes away by bus ride. There were orgy houses, where a person could pay $25 to get in and have sex with anyone they saw including someone's wife. California was wild and out-of-control, therefore; I stayed to my boring Indiana ways, watching TV, playing an occasional game of basketball, or spending time in the gym. I stayed in the barracks so long I was beginning to get cabin fever. I just couldn't eat one more burrito from the roach coach or watch one more episode of Gomer pile, I had to get out of the barracks and out into life.

A DAY OF NORMALCY

Saturday morning I decide to venture out in town early, I put 20 bucks in my pocket, just enough for a round trip bus ride to and from base and possibly some lunch. I tuck the rest of my money inside of a book hidden in the top of my wall locker, I had a safe proof lock, so I thought. I watch the commercials of a lock being shot with a rifle and still didn't open, until one Marine demonstrated how quickly he can get through my lock with one slap of his hammer, so I relocated my money to another spot, I lifted my bed up and remove the stopper at the base of the bed post, then I shoved my money up the pole of my bed, and off to Oceanside I went. I walked around the town endlessly looking in the store windows, hanging out on the beach or just watching people as part of my weekend fun, finally I went into the barbershop to get my weekly haircut.

This was something new for me, I had never been to a barbershop where all the barbers were white males. I was unsure about the outcome, but I thought, "Marines only wear regulation high and tight haircuts, so it really doesn't matter how the haircut turns out. When he was done he handed me a mirror to check out the back of my head, I noticed a ball spot beginning to form in the center of my scalp, indicating the first signs of alopecia. I was horrified at the possibility of going bald. I must have sat in the chair for two minutes looking in the mirror while rubbing the small spot on the back of my head.

I couldn't stay there all day so I jumped out of the chair, gave the barber five dollars and out to the sunny streets of Oceanside I went. The streets were jam-packed with young marines and young attractive prostitutes relieving them of their hard earned pay. It was a total culture shock, not like Indianapolis restricted by color. In California more than just black-and-white populated the city, the population of California was well mixed, women from different cultures with long beautiful black hair stretching down their back. The women laid openly on the beaches in their skimpy bathing suits. I thought I had found a part of heaven, walking along the beach with my tongue dragging in the sand looking at all the beautiful expos bodies as far as the eye can see.

The bordom of the base was overwhelming, five 12 hour days of looking at cannon tubes stretching towards the sky outlined by the plus green rolling hills alongside los pogas road. I couldn't stand it anymore so I jumped on the bus and headed to May Company Mall. There was a young girl on the bus sitting directly across from me, her long athletic legs we're covered with stockings that had runs in them, I didn't care I worked around men all day, five days week, therefore; this was a sight to behold. She wore a black mini-skirt with a tight white T-shirt displaying her well proportioned torso.

She stared at me for a while then struck up a conversation, before I knew it we were walking around the mall together shopping. She couldn't have been more than 18 years old or the same age as I. We walked and talk for hours prosing through several stores, I was becoming quite comfortable with her, stepping close behind her while she looked at his shirts and pants, I seductively assisted her by holding pants to her waistline while she looked over her shoulder into the mirror. I was in hog heaven, I haven't been this close to a woman in months, and I had to say it did feel good. I stayed with her that day for about five hours, looking at stockings, jewelry, and miscellaneous items of furniture. I walked closely behind her heading towards the register so she could purchase a new pair of Black stockings.

She lead me into a part of the mall I've never been, then she walked into a secluded corner of the mall placing one hand on my shoulder to bounce her weight, she reached up her skirt and pull off her stockings, "Hold on to these" she said laying the stockings on my shoulder, I can still smell the perfume dropping from her once saturated stocking. She remove her new stockings from the packet , putting one leg at a time in each stocking then pulling the panty hose up.

She wasn't wearing a stitch of underwear, her skin was smooth and soft as cotton. I felt light headed and unresponsive, I was just beginning to go into starvation mode when she suggested going to lunch. I stood there in a daze staring at her, I could see her mouth moving but I wasn't hearing anything, she snapped her fingers and patted me on the side of my face saying, "Come on, let's go eat". "I know the perfect place". She grabbed me by the hand, her soft female touch maded me drool slightly but I stayed in control and off we went back into the mall. She walk ed slightly in front of me pulling me down the hallways of the mall as if I was her boyfriend or husband. I purposely linger behind her trying to catch a glimpse of those long Beautiful thin legs covered with $1.98 stockings.

The restaurant was beautiful, white table cloths covering every table with fancy napkins made into the shape of animals, with a candle burning brightly in the center of each table. "What was I doing in a place like this"? I thought to myself. I began to feel awkward and out of place, because I barely had enough money to pay for my own meal and I always felt it was the man's job to pay for the meal, so I told her to give me a second, then I ditched around the corner, I begin counting my money, I had $11 dollars to my name, I was so embarrassed I could only afford to pay for my meal, and definitely knew I couldn't pay for hers. We sat down to lunch, I scooted her chair under her trying to be a total gentleman, it was my first time using an actual menu, I knew I was in a financial dilemma.

I scoured the menu quickly with my eyes, the cheapest thing on the menu was a tuna melt sandwich and it cost seven dollars without fries, even the water was a dollar a glass. I frantically calculated the taxes in my head, my meal cost slightly less then I had in my pocket, I had another 1.50 stuffed in my socks but I wouldn't dare use it because it was my only means of transportation back to the base.

She could see the trepidation on my face, she reached across the table and delicately touched my hand, "We can go Dutch." She said. I squinted my eyes indicating I was confused, "We can each pay for our own meal" she said. I internally let go of a side of relief, my vertebrae was no longer locked into position and I was finally able to swallow the lump in my throat. She ordered a huge meal costing somewhere around $15, I felt naked, sitting there with my paltry little tuna melt sandwich with garnishment decorating the plate.

I pretended as though I hated fries, keeping the price of the meal down to save myself the embarrassment when the check came, so I played it smart and just ordered a tuna fish sandwich, and ten cent more I added a slice of cheese try not to show that I was totally broke. She sat in front of me with a huge platter of food forking it down, not even catching her breath between bites. She ate fast like she was in boot camp, I nibbled around the edges of my tuna fish sandwich taking my time trying to make it last. I stared across the table at her slim, perfectly built frame, fantasizing about the possibility of a sexual encounter.

We talked for an hour and seemingly grew comfortable enough with one another to talk about our heritage and where we were from. She said she was from East LA, she is Hispanic, she grow up in a dysfunctional family plague by gangs and violence. She needed to get away from the violence of her everyday life that's why she moved to Oceanside California. I'd begin to feel a sense of friendship developing between us, the thought of pulling slick moves to get close to her dissipated from my mind. I gave her space, not even trying to slip my hand around her beautiful thin waist.

Eventually we caught another bus back to Oceanside Boulevard where she lead me into a pool hall filled with young Marines smoking cigarettes and drinking beer, the last place I wanted to be was around a bunch of jar heads. She seemed very popular and right at home as she made her rounds greeting everyone she saw, everyone in the pool hall knew her, a few men walked up to her, picked her up and kissed her on the jaw.

Several man proposition her for dates later in the evening, before accepting, she looked over her shoulder at me then back to business as usual. I observed her for a few more minutes and all of a sudden it hit me, she was a prostitute. I quietly slipped out of pool hall and walked down to hoagies corner and purchased a .50 cent piece of beef jerky to snack on for the bus ride back to the base. I climbed onto the first bus and Stared out the window thinking about my day as the bus twisted and turned down Los pogus dark winding road. It was a long quiet ride, only two other Marines occupy the bus because it was still early in the day, most Marines didn't return to the base until the last bus left Oceanside at 12:30 in the evening. I sat in the back of the bus trying to get clarity about what just happened. I came to the understanding that this young girl just wanted too feel normal for one day. Maybe she want to experience what it was like for other girls her same age who wasn't dating for money or being offered money for sex. I believe this was the closest she would come to feeling normal. This was the first time in months that I had an intimate relationship with the female, a woman's soft touch and the smell of her perfume came home like truth.

It had been seven months since I've visited Indianapolis as well as several months since I had sex. I was 19 years old and horny as hell. I had trouble sleeping at night. I was fine doing daylight hours because I was preoccupied with my job as a Cannoneer. But when the night fell I was alone and didn't have anything to deterred me from thinking about 29th & Talbott.

Every Friday evening we were released to go to chow then return to begin cleaning the barracks. We scrubbed and polish the bathroom floors for three hours before the first inspection. A tall squared away brass lieutenant walked in as though he was inspecting the barracks at the eighth and I duty station in Washington DC. He rubbed his hand across the wall and under the bathroom sinks, pulling one finger out with less than a microfiber of dust. He said, "It's not clean, continue to field day and call me when its ready.

Everyone was thoroughly pissed off, the lieutenant want to play mine fuck games and keep us cleaning the bathrooms all night. After two more hours of thoroughly cleaning the barracks, scrubbing walls, scrubbing in and behind the toilet, we fell we are ready for another inspection, so we sent the runner to summons the lieutenant. He strutted down the hallway of the barracks, belching from the pastrami sandwich he just finished. He walked in the bathroom look at the roll of toilet paper, "It's too thin", he said, "replace the roll and call me when you're done'. He strutted out the door as though he owned the world. We replace all the Rolls of toilet paper in the stall, we sprayed Windex on the toilets to give them a nice shine and the appearance of being brand-new.

We used our tooth brushes and scrub around the edge of the toilets in any visible seam, we sent a runner into town to purchase civilian bathroom cleaning products, after three more hours of cleaning and scrubbing we sent for the lieutenant. By this time it was 1 AM in the morning, the lieutenant strutted down the hallway as fresh as he was at 5 PM, not a hair out of place. I stood back and observe as he bent down on one knee and wiped his finger around the edge of the toilet, lifting the seat off the toilet he turned and said "this toilet is not clean".

Sgt. said, "Pardon me sir the toilet is clean". "Well, Sgt. This toilet is not clean, and you just failed another inspection, I'll come back at 4 AM." The lieutenant said. The sergeant said," sir if I can proof the toilet is clean would you releases us for the night. "how are you going to prove that" said the Lieut. The Sgt. got Down on one knee, reaching into the bowl with both hands, he scooped out water from the toilet and drink the water from his hands. The lieutenant looked shockingly at the Sgt. and said, you're secure for the night. It was almost 2 o'clock in the morning, the buses were no longer running on the base. I think everyone was too tired to chase women are go bar hopping, we all return to our rooms for a night of well earned sleep.

Saturday mornings were the best of all it was one of few days the Marine Corps didn't bother us. So I cruised over to the chow hall before catching the bus to San Diego to see a movie. I thought a movie would help distract my thoughts from any sexual desires but the movie had two sexual scenes that had me reeling from the theater in search of a drugstore where I can purchase some type of prophylactic for a possible night of sexual ecstasy. Right after the movie I decided to cruise the San Diego strip.

I was one block away from the theater before being quickly approached by a young white girl, she was around 25 years old with dirty blond hair, she was a "BWG" Basic white girl with a nondescript body. She looked and smelled different from the girls I grew up with. The girls at my high school smelled like pickles and Kool-Aid a popular snack in the 70s, the girls carried pickles and Kool-Aid strews in their purses providing themselves with a snack in a moments notice.

The pickles looked as though there on steroids, they were large and sealed in a plastic bag with juice. The kook-aid strews were long at least 24 inches hosting several different flavors. This girl was different, not only was she from a different ethnic group her blond hair was straight and lifeless, not possessing any body, curl or style. She wreaked of cigarette smoke and seemed very overt and aggressive as She walked upon me fast as if she was trying to beat someone else to the punch, she said, "I am the best" I looked at her with a confused look on my face and said "you're the best at what"? she paused for a second looked at me squinting her eyes while taking a long drag from her cigarette.

If I didn't know better I would think she was rehearsing for a Humphrey Bogart movie. "I'm the best at giving head" she said. "you're a cop" I implied, and I don't have any time to sit in jail". She looked at me with astonishment and said "I'm not a cop! Just ask the other women around" so I made my way up and down the strip checking her credentials, after 10 minutes of asking questions while observing her from a distance I discover she was telling the truth she wasn't a cop.

I slowly marched towards her at a half step. I leaned over and whispered in her ear.

"How much,?" She said, "It will cost you $20". " I don't have $20" I said while frantically searching through my wallet.

"How much do you have?" She said.

"I have $14 dollars to my name.' I said as the dollar and fifty cent shifted around in my scoks. She looked at me disappointedly rolling her eyes.

"That's okay, it's enough to buy me a pack of cigarettes, let's go" she said.

We jumped into a yellow taxi heading around the corner just a little more than a mile to her house. I was creeped out by the entire seen but I was being lead blindly by my emotional horny state.

I didn't have a clear thought in my head, I was being controlled by my little head not my big head which made me forget about any possible dangers that may have lurked inside of her house. Her room was a very basic set up just for business. A full-size bed shoved in the corner, of the living room. A cheap night table and a lamp without a shade using a low wattage bulb that played havoc on my eyes. After my 10 minutes of non-passionate lust I quickly got dressed and started jogging back to the bus station before the last bus departed to Oceanside.

2500 MILES AWAY FROM HOME

After weeks and weeks of dreaming about going home, July arrived and before I knew it I was 35,000 feet in the air catching jet lag. Over the course of seven months our relationship thrived only on letters and postcards, continuously building on a relationship of infatuation rather than love. I hung out at her house day and night, her mother never requested that I leave but she listened throughout tonight to ensure that Cindy didn't slip back down stairs. Unfortunately for her we were young so we did what people do, we fell into the age-old trap of lust and desire. At two in the morning Cindy found her way downstairs and into my arms for the night.

We spent the next 15 days hanging out at the park, walking, talking, and holding hands where time and space permitted. Cindy love material possessions, and felt since I was her boyfriend I was supposed to buy her a $400 stereo system. I have just under $300 dollars to my name but I reluctantly gave it to her in hopes it would fill the empty void missing in her happiness. But she was thoroughly pissed off because I was $100.00 dollars short, so she tossed the money back to me and went home. I felt kind of bad about the whole thing, about her not being able to buy her stereo but I didn't feel bad enough to give her the money again, I purchase a tens sack of white castles and a large chocolate shake. Conscious clear I sat on my mothers patio and wished I didn't have to return to the base, but before I knew it my leave was over I had to return to camp Pendleton.

My 15 days of leave came to a bitter end, I grab and hug Cindy before reluctantly boarding the 747 airplane. I walked down the lonely 30 foot ramp and Took my seat in the coach section of the plane. I raise and lower the window shade on the plane several times signaling goodbye. Everyone else walked away hurrying to the car to claim the shotgun seat ride back home, my mother stayed until the plane back out onto the tarmac, once the plane was in the air she went to her car. I sat on the plane looking forlorn with my face pressed against the window staring at the open sky. The stewardess notice my uniform and the lone look on my face, so she walked over and ask if I wanted to sit in first class. I looked up at her holding back my tears I could barely speak but I was able to say,

"No thank you".

I knew I had made a mistake enlisting in the corp for four years. I missed my family, and my friends, it was a part of my life that I could never get back, watching my siblings grow up and my mother gracefully age to the person she became to today. I could feel the distance widening between us as the plane climbed to 30,000 feet. Four years of family memories that would never be realized, only memories of myself and the men I served with in the core.

CHOCOLATE MOUNTAIN

I reported back to my unit and was told to pack my gear, we're heading out to Chocolate Mountain Arizona. We loaded our trucks with axes, pics, shovels, a huge camouflage net, personal weapons including an M-60 caliber machine gun and a 50 caliber anti aircraft weapon. We hitched our cannons to the back of the 5 ton trucks and stage them at the gun park. We stood in formation to listen to a one hour lecture on safety, don't play with the rattle snakes, don't pick up unexploded ordinance, they told us not to do all of the things they knew Marines would do.

The next morning we were off, rolling through the Beautiful neighborhoods of Fallbrook lined with orange trees touching every bend of the road. Out the gate and down the highway at 60 miles an hour dragging 15,500 pound cannons behind us, trucks stretching 2 miles long down the highway. The ride was long, sweltering heat and hard wooden benches made it very difficult to enjoy the scenic view. Seabags where stack celling high in the back of the truck, the locker meant for storing tools was jam packed with pokey bait, extra food Marines bring to the field to keep from eating C-rations. We became very creative in our boredom, we ripped apart cardboard boxes and wrote messages asking women to pull their shirts up displaying their breasts. Screams could be heard from the last truck all the way to the leading truck as the civilian women pass by exposing their breast.

Two marines riding alongside me in the back of our truck begin to argue. The white guy repeatedly called the Cuban guy Fidel. They were almost at blows, so I position myself between them to keep the argument from escalating into a fight. It was all I could do to prevent them from destroying the back of the truck. Later that evening we arrived at chocolate Mountain Arizona. It was seven at night and still

100° in the shade, no one was allowed to bunk down until all the vehicles and equipment were prepare for the training exercise. Setting up our nets on top of the trucks, reorganizing the back of the trucks making ready for rapid exit, and making room for loading 100 live artillery shells, and stacking case after case of C-rations, as well as four, 5 gallon cans of water.

The next morning I was awaken by the sound of Diesel fuel coming from trucks reviving their engines, thick Gray smoke poured from their stacks, "Amtrak's" amphibious assault vehicles and tanks were the first to pull out, artillery follow close behind. The infantry hit the ground running the same day we arrived, they never stopped humping until they marched 10 miles beyond the artillery and tank units. After hours of driving we took position in a desolate place in the middle of nowhere.

I was given a 5 gallon can of water, a case of C-Rations and a prick radio. I was told to guard the road and not allow anyone to come within 5 miles of the live fire zone. I was left in that desolate part of the desert by myself for four days without seeing another human being. I spent my nights staring at the sky full of stars thinking about Cindy and what she was doing. I spend my days trying to be creative and use my poncho to deflect the sun, trying to stay out of the direct sun light and the sweltering heat.

My fourth day guarding the road I became extremely bored, so I begin to do all the things the Marine Corps told us not to do. I looked for snakes, poking and prodding in the holes hoping to force him out the backside. While walking I nearly tripped over a 500 pound unexploded bomb dropped by one of our Navy Jets. I backed up very slowly, placing 1 foot behind the other delicately on the ground until I was nearly 100 paces away. I grab my prick radio and reported the unexploded shell. Jeeps fill with ordnance personnel appeared out of no-where as though they rolled right out of the sand. I was transported to the top of a hill and watch as the ordinance crew placed C4 and Primacor wrapped around the unexploded shell and destroying the Shell and everything within 50 meters of it. An hour later I was returned to my unit, my skin was three shades darker than when I left.

I couldn't help but smile from ear to ear as I toss my gear into the back of the truck and squatted down next to the tire to prepare a stove to heat my C-rations, just as my food was warming up I heard a loud explosion. Everyone stood up at once trying to get a fix on what direction the explosion came from. We could see smoke coming from 150 yards away then all of a sudden a navy jet broke through the clouds, swooping down on top of us dropping another shell, a little closer this time within 125 yards of our position.

Scrap metal spray the area, ripping through the truck tarps and piercing the metal on the truck doors. Capt. Moore grab the prick Radio and try to call for cease-fire as the third Navy jet flipped it's wing to the right turning the corner. Everyone was running for their life, but there was no where to hide in the vast flat land of the desert. I tried to hide behind the ordinance on the ground but the shells were falling to close to the trucks to take cover, so we ran as far and as fast as we could from the drop zone before the third Shell hit the ground. Three Marines were hit with strap metal and one Marine jumped on a cactus bush. I lay behind a telephone pole that somehow ended up in the middle of the desert.

I bury my face deep in the sand, I could hear the strap metal hitting the pole and grazing the top of my helmet, just as we thought it was safe another jet turned the corner with its engine roaring. The jet was ahead of its sound but this time I looked straight at the Jet coming down right on top of us preparing to drop another 500 pound shell, my commanding officer grab a Smoke grenade and toss it as far as he could Into the drop zone, the Jets saw the smoke and pulled away from our position.

The scrap metal from the 500 lbs pound shell disable two of the cannons, flatting their tires and shattering the wind shields of several trucks, therefore; myself and another Marine was put on a truck and sent to the rear to guard the ammo dump. I reluctantly grab my gear and dragged it over to the ammo dump where I spent the next two days with the sun beating directly down on my head, there was no cover, we weren't allowed to put up a tent because the helicopters would come in and kick up so much sand and wind it will pull the tents out of the ground and rip them into shred. So we sat there in the sweltering and blistering sun reluctantly getting a complete body tan that I didn't need.

We had only been in the desert a week and already my skin was looking dry and brittle, my lips were chapped and cracking and the lip balm and Vaseline provided little relief. The winds were picking up making little sand twisters less than a foot from the stacks of ammunition. There was news of a possible sand storm heading our way, only the news had arrived two minutes too late, I couldn't see 1 foot in front of me and within minutes our cannons were practically buried up to the top of the tires, all the low ranking personnel we're forced to walk guard duty, standing outside in the middle of the storm protecting equipment that no civilian knew was even there. We rotated shifts three hours on and 3 off, no one really stayed awake during the twilight hours, they just pass the fire watch list, watch and flashlight on to the next fire watch. I had the 2 AM to 4 AM shift, I love being awake doing the twilight hours when everyone else was asleep.

I was totally exhausted from the days activities and Quickly fell into a deep sleep. Someone tap me on the shoulder then handed me the flashlight and watch. I shined the flash light on the watch to check the time, I rolled over and just stayed in my sleeping bag until my shift ended. Wearing nothing but boots, a T-shirt and camouflage utilities I walked 25 meters to the other Canon and handed the watch and flashlight to the next person on patrol. I turned around and took 10 paces and realized I couldn't see 1 foot in front of me, I wave my hand back-and-forth less than an inch in front of my face. I couldn't see my hand because it was pitch black.

I yelled out to the Marines sleeping around my Canon but there was no response, so I walked in the direction from which I came and still I couldn't see anyone so I squatted down trying to see an outline of a truck or tent but there was nothing there. So I yelled out once again and once again no one respond, so I begin walking in the direction I thought I came from, I must have walk around for more than an hour believing I was walking around my units location but I was at least five or 6 miles down the road where the amphibious assault vehicle division was located, so I kept walking. Freezing cold from the bitter night air, my leather boots felt hard as rocks because of the cold weather and the absence of wearing socks.

The further I walked the further I was moving away from my unit. I look down and saw grunts lying in their two man fighting positions. I knew I had gone too far so I did a 180 and went back in the other direction. More than an hour and a half past and I was finally back to my unit. I located some Communication wire in the middle of our camp clearly marked and leading to each Canon. I figured out which wire lead to my Canon so I traced the wire all the way back to my Canon then lifelessly lay down on my cot, closed my eyes for 10 minutes before reveille was sounded. I was exhausted and my misfortune was, we just began a three day no sleep training exercise that morning. We moved non-stop all day and silently into the night dragging our cannons behind us kicking up nose clogging dust, only stopping temporarily to bell from the trucks when the navy Jets flew overhead spraying us with CS gas.

The Marines moved hard and fast stopping occasionally to perform hip shoots, then back on the trucks. The other days were spent performing Hilo raids, pushing the small 105 cannons into the back of helicopters then landing for approximately five minutes, firing off two artillery shells then back in the helicopter to repeat the same raids over and over again until it was time for night fire. The roads were long and hot, I could see heat waves in the distance covering the vast empty desert. As miserable as I was I couldn't help but to have occasional thought of Cindy and what she was doing at the moment.

My euphoric thoughts were interrupted by more CS gas and the 120° temperature inside my mop suit. The water drinking device on my gas mask didn't work so I had to go for hours without water because they didn't allow us to remove the gas mask until all clear was given. It was like a scene out of a war movie. As far as the eye can see trucks were lined up along the desert road and the Navy pilots couldn't help but to spray us with their gas one last time as we headed to base camp.

We jumped off the trucks and scatter in all directions pointing our weapons in the air and firing blanks at the jets while trying to Don our gas mask and cover ourselves with ponchos to stop the burning effect of the CS gas. Immediately after all clear was given two Marines ran from the road Down into a huge crater and begin hitting each other with shovels and tent poles and what ever else within their reach. Marines stood around the top of the crater taking bets as the two Marines bludgeoned themselves half to death until one Marine Cpl. Step in and ended the fight. It was the two Marines I prevented from fighting in the back of the truck on the way to the desert, they finally had enough of one another and decided to settle the difference "Marine Corps" style.

The fight was soon forgotten and before we knew it we were on our way back to camp Pendleton. The ride home wasn't as much fun because dirt soaked deep into the pores of our skin, we choked and threw up in the back of the trucks from remnants of sand caught in our throats and particles of sand trap in the corner folds of our eyes, that sealed our eyes shut. We had not bathed for eight weeks and the C-Rations give off an awful smell while Marines try to cleanse their Colon. Grunting and clutching onto the bathroom stall because they were constipation from the military diet of C-rations.

In the Marines we were supposedly guaranteed one hot meal and one hour of sleep per day doing combat conditions, but we never saw the Hot meal and scarcely saw one hour of sleep during training. I often thought of Cindy and what she's doing and whether or not she thought of me as often as I thought of her. We were young and in the mist of puppy love, I often thought about the way we were. I wished I were more mature and prepared for what was about to take place in my life, I hadn't experienced anything compelling or jolting to my character, I have yet to be tested, but I rest assure the test was coming.

A FALL FROM GRACE

I was back in the barracks and could easily find time during the quiet hours of the night to write Cindy letters but to my surprise I was selected for (NCO) noncommissioned officer school where corporals and sergeants went to be groomed for leadership. I was not yet an NCO I was just an E-3 with less than a year in the Corps, the leadership school was eight weeks, a modified version of Boot Camp, fast-paced with a lot of physical activity. There were more than 50 Marines in the leadership school and I was the only E-3 in the entire class. I feel so out of place and so overwhelmed it wasn't long before the corporals and sergeants try to place me on every shit detail they could create, but they were easily reminded that pulling rank wasn't an option at the school but they plotted and through obstacles in my way, trying to find ways to drop me from the program.

From the very first inspection I would receive unwarranted demerits that other Marines receive a pass on. We were separated into nine man squads no one want to be in the squad with an E-3, they had no choice but to allow me to participate but they didn't make it easy. I was placed with eight other Marines that could run 3 miles in 17 minutes. I wasn't the slowest runner at the time my best 3 mile run was 21 minutes. During the final three weeks of NCO school we had a squad run competition, we were the last squad to started the 6 mile course, by the time we reached 3 miles we passed all the other squads and was ahead of them by at least three minutes.

Four miles into the run one of our corporals fell behind, the pace was very excruciating, we were running at a six minute mile pace, my knees begin to feel pressure from the uphill, downhill interchange, causing me to fall back 5 feet from my squad. The other marine fell back more than 50 yards causing the squad to slowdown so that he could catch up. Finally we made it back to the barracks after a 6 mile grueling fast-paced run. Everyone blamed me for the other Marine Inability to keep up with the squad. They said,

"If you hadn't drop back he would've run harder to keep up".

Only one Marine came to my defense, saying that "it was bullshit and it wasn't my fault that the other Marine fell behind". I knew I was being targeted for blame and it wouldn't be long before I was dropped from NCO school.

It has been six weeks and I could see the finish line but later that evening I received a letter from Cindy. She reluctantly informed me she was pregnant and her mother was very upset and threatening to call my commanding officer if I didn't marry her. Personally I could give a flying bat butt about her mother being upset, I was more concerned about becoming a father. That night I rode the city bus Down to Oceanside Boulevard. I walked into one of their sleazy bars, they could tell by my high and tight haircut that I was a jar head and even though I was only 19 they allow me to drink my problems away.

I was so distraught by the information of becoming a father, I lost my focus and could not longer study, therefore; I was put out of the (NCO) noncommissioned officer program doing the Final two weeks before graduation. I was embarrassed to return to my unit, because I was a failure but I had bigger fish to fry. I had a child on the way and soon a wife, there wasn't any way I was going to let Cindy have my baby unwedded, and my infatuation for her slowly turned into love. In the month of October I receive orders to go overseas to Okinawa Japan the following year, January 5, 1980, and I was given 30 days leave before shipping out. December 1, I landed in Indianapolis, my first stop was my mothers house, then across the bridge I walk to Cindy's house. Her mother answer the door and said," Cindy is in the kitchen".

I walked towards the kitchen and in a flash she ran down into the basement then out the side door. She was reluctant to let me see her stomach protruding pass her unfasten blue jeans. So I sat nonchalantly on the living room couch . The couch was cover with plastic, if it were hot outside I surely would have been on my way to dehydration. I waited patiently for Cindy to collect her self, she was being obnoxiously shy, but I understood, so I sat on the couch until she walked into the room and set down beside me. I reached over opened her coat and rub her stomach, at that exact time I knew I loved her and I couldn't allow her to be an unwedded mother, I stared deep into her eyes while running my fingers through her hair and once again she became soft and melted into my arms.

She cried and I whisper softly in her ear "Would you be my wife"? She "yes".

We sat a date for December 29, 1979, at Stouffer's Inn a very prestigious hotel less than a mile from my mothers house. I took my last nine hundred dollars and paid for the ballroom and catering, Cindy and her close friend was in charge of the decorations, the room appeared very Idyllic, many of the wedding party were not particularly interested in the wedding themselves, but attended the wedding to observe firsthand the oulchritudinous view of the ballroom. Around 50 people were in attendance for the wedding including my grandmother. Seeing her at my wedding pleased me to see her out and about rather than sitting in the kitchen gossiping with my aunt. Cindy and I were both so young, barely out of high school, naïve, and very uncertain about raising a child. I stood on the left when I should've been on the right which caused me to place the ring on the wrong finger. I just wanted this process over with and to get on with my life.

While everyone else ate cake and slow danced to songs by Earth wind and fire. I slipped away into far off places, thoughts of living in Japan settle quietly into my murky subconscious. Everyone seemed to be having a good time until Cindy's stepfather began complaining about the food and how little he was able to get. As quiet as it was kept I spent my last $900 to have the food catered, but Cindy's mother took credit for paying for the food and the ball room. By the time the rumor made it back to me about who pay for the food and ballroom I didn't care, I just want the night to come to an end. Cindy and I was whisked away to my brothers small two bedroom house where we would spend the first 24 hours of our marriage. We were reluctant to stay but unfortunately we were short on funds and didn't have many other options, therefore we agreed to stay the night but within an hour we were bifurcate into disagreeable factions. Here we were one hour into the marriage and already had our first fight. Cindy set in the bedroom trying to codify our life while I stared aimlessly out the front window trying to grasp the fact that I will be more than 12,000 miles away within five days.

I believe that's truly what the fight was about. Before I knew it I was sitting on the plane with my face pressed against the airplane window trying to get a glimpse of my pregnant wife as the plane back out onto the tarmac. The fight was overcrowded and It was just my luck to sit next to an obese women wreaking of cheap perfume. I was being mentally tormented, covering my nose with a wet handkerchief, the smell was worse than CS gas because we were in a closed off area. The 22 hour flight laid over in Anchorage Alaska for one and a half hours, then onto Guam airport, a small building, less than 2000 Ft.[2]. A barracuda hanging lifelessly on the wall displaying all of its teeth trying to provide some sense of art and style in the dainty little airport. Pictures of the island hung freely on the walls telling the history of the island and the battle it took to keep the island. Two hours into my layover we boarded the plane for our final destination, Okinawa Japan. I was fortunate to arrive while the sun was still high in the sky. I sat pensively internally feeling the distance from home with every screeching sound of the airplane wheels touching down on the runway. I wasn't comfortable being in another country, so I stuck close to the base my first two months on the island. Occasionally I walked around the perimeter of the fence getting a feel for what it was like to be in a Japanese neighborhood. The houses were close together one right on top of the other with a small side walk between two tiny houses. Vendors stood on every corner selling sushi and other types of exotic seafood. I thought the people were very pleasant, more so than the foreigners that assimilated while living in the US. I ran around the island like an idiot with a Japanese translation hand book yelling "mushy mushy," meaning hello hello. Once a person stopped to talk to me I thumb through the book for something else to say but they always walked off before I could find the next phrase.

I stayed very close to the barracks, bored out of my mind I watch Japanese cartoons, 'Transformers' in their language. I didn't understand a thing, all the street signs were in Japanese and the streets ran in the opposite direction of the US. I searched the newspaper for criminal activity, picking up a word here and there. I was totally frustrated and felt out of place, culture shock begin to creep in and before I knew it I was shipped to Korea for cold-weather training (Jack Frost) a training exercise conducted yearly throughout the entire fleet Marine force (FMF Pack).

I was tired and want to sleep but I was thrown into a group of Marines and marched to the nearest supply room and began withdrawing my sub-standard cold weather training gear. I arrived in Korea 5 days later and was immediately escorted to a Government personnel tent (GP) where 80 other Marines were suffering the same faith as I. We were living in the chosen frozen, fortunately for us it was the Cold War Era. South Korea was at peace but North Korea maintain a threatening presence just on the other side of the fence line, marines were stretched out along the demobilizing zone (DMZ) to prevent the occupying North Korea forces from crossing into the forbidden zone.

Most nights the temperatures plummet into -30°. All I could do to stay warm was put two rocks on the pub stoves to get them hot, then place the rocks in the foot of my sleeping bag to prevent my feet from turning into walking ice planks. The ceiling of the tent was covered with 12 inch icicles that hung desperately close to our face as we lay sleeping in our ill-equipped cold weather sleeping bags. I woke at 4:00 and made my way outside to the tent covered bathroom just 15 meters from our sleeping quarters. I was thoroughly disgusted by the bathroom facility. The toilets were knee high, making it difficult to mount and have a seat. Before we could take a dump, we had to remove three layers of clothes, including a parka and snow boots. Frozen Feces cover the top of all the toilets from one end of the bathroom to the other, there was at least 10 toilets, two rolls with five toilets on each side. The toilets were wooden with no supporting back structure, we had to lean against the person behind us or squat on top of the toilet which is what most Marines did according to the evidence they left sitting on top of the toilet. Every morning a maintenance crew with high pressure steam sprayers tried to clean the bathroom using a water hose and scrub brushes, the feces would just liquefied then freeze on top of the toilet leaving a brown slippery residue.

Most Marines got fully undressed so they could balance themselves while taking a dump, there was no place to hang your clothes so we had to be very creative each time we visit the latrine. Holding our clothes in our hand while slipping and sliding on the ice cover rice patties. The Marines believe in teamwork and this was teamwork at its best. Two men had to travel to the latrine together to assist one another with completing their morning ritual of pinching a loaf. I became so frustrated with the process I grabbed a shovel and begin searching for a secluded place bordering the camp, about 100 meters from my tent was the Air Force campsite. I wanted to see for myself how nice they lived, up to this point I only heard rumors about them living like civilians. So I creeped over to the nearest Air Force building then peek inside. I couldn't believe how nice their bathrooms were, mirrors on the wall, clean porcelain toilets with wooden floors, and not to mention the bathroom was fully heated. I couldn't believe it, Paradise in the wilderness.

At last I could drop my pants lay back against the porcelain toilet seat and pinch a loaf as though I was in the civilian world. Although I was in the Air Force plush bathroom, the 12 weeks of C-rations had worked its Magic. It did exactly what it was designed to do, it made me constipated preventing me from pinching a loaf at will. I hated going to the bathroom it was a very painful and unpleasant experience. Although I only had to go to the bathroom once every three weeks I hated stripping down totally naked just to cleanse my colon. Once I discovered the dietary purpose of C-rations, I stop eating what the military gave me in exchange for carrying my own pokey bait. Food that we purchased from the PX, such as tuna, ramen noodle, cookies, crackers, and other canned goods. I went hungry for my first three weeks in Korea because Lance Cpl. Bird was assigned to mess duty, he would get up at 2 AM and crack eggs all morning long. He was so agitated by the process and pissed off at the world he mix the egg shells in with the eggs, ruining everyone's breakfast.

The bacon was frozen solid, smothered with frozen grease resembling vasaline. it took several napkins to wiped away the grease before we could eat it, the coffee was the safest bet, pure black and steaming hot. No one in the unit liked Bird, he was a class A jerk, so they send him as far away from our unit as they could. They assigned him to work on shit details just to keep him away from us. Bird was a compulsive liar, he would tell grandiose lies about owning a home on a rotating mountain, people was sick of listening to his lies, everytime he came around we just walked away.

All of the training and living conditions were very harsh in the Marine Corps, even the showers were run by generators, there was no way for the operators to control the temperature, scalding hot water was piped through tubes attached to a rod coming from the generator, it was as if we were lobsters being boiled in a pot, wooden shipping pallets were used for floors. The floors were so cold the hundred degree hot steaming water couldn't prevent the wooden pallets from being covered with ice.

Even the dressing area entrance to the showers were rice patties covered with ice. Everywhere we stepped there was ice under our feet, it didn't matter how hot the shower water would get the ice just wouldn't melt. Every morning for 12 weeks marines crowded around the small pot stove sucking up all the heat before it could reach anyone else. I couldn't believe how stupid I was getting myself in this type of situation it should be a crime to be so stupid. I couldn't get the fact out of my head that the Air Force camp was just 100 meters across the grinder. They were living a life of luxury in plush two man tent's with real wooden floors, not shipping pallets.

They had dressers with the mirrors attached and drawers to put their clothes in and a civilian maded quilt covering their beds. I envied and I hated them at the same time. Our lifestyles were totally different but our mission was the same, 'keep the North Koreans in the North'. I spent 12 weeks sleeping on ice covered rice patties, pulling icicles from the ceiling of our tent, using them for water to make coffee. I never drink pure black coffee before this experience, but it was so cold, adding milk or creamer wasn't a secondary thought. I just wanted something hot to drink, I didn't care what it taste like. I couldn't imagine fighting a war in these type of conditions as the Marines did who came before us. It didn't matter how cold it was there was always something to do outside in that horrid weather conditions. We parked our cannons in rice fields of some poor farmer, his home was less than 100 hundred meters away from our firing positions, we didn't care whether it kept him up all night so we shot our live artillery shells over the City highway onto desolate land designated as the live fire zone.

We stood on the firing line for hours in 30° below weather with a windchill factor of 25 mph waiting for a fire mission, the fire missions came few and far between and by 3 o'clock that evening someone got the bright idea to rotate the gun crews every couple hours. We stood out on the firing line until 10 pm at night, my eye sockets were just about frozen in place and my mouth had frozen stiff. I could barley pronounce words or talk. As it got later in the evening Bush bunnies made their presence known, whispering from the bush "GI GI Fucking sucky $10". I just kept walking my post pretending not to notice them but some Marines couldn't resist the temptation of having sex with the young girls, they gladly jumped into the bushes for a cheap thrill that turned out to be a very painful visit to the dispensary. Bush girls weren't tested by the military for sexually transmitted diseases.

Prostitution was legal in the bars of Soul Korea, therefore; the military insured that the women occupying the bars got routine physicals or vaccinated the venereal diseases. If the girls refused to be tested by the military the business owner would have to place a pile of Salt on either side of the door alerting young soldiers, sailors, and Marines to the presence of sexually transmitted diseases within that establishment. I was married and didn't want to take any chances on the possibility of spreading any diseases to my wife so I stayed away from the Bush bunnies and the bars for the time being. Most of the time I didn't think about sex because it was so cold in South Korea I couldn't occupy another thought in my head other than how to get warm.

Once we return back to our base camp for a weekend of R&R I found solace just laying on my cot, my toes were just about frost bitten, frozen with a painful tingling and needle pricking sensation as though I had the sickle cell trait. The doctors were busy treating high-ranking officers, therefore; I was requisite to be examined by a Navy Corpmans with no formal education, rather he had an quick eight week training course in the medical field. Several hundred of us suffered the same predicament while overwhelming the two corpsmen in their small CP tent.

I still had feeling in my feet and the ability to work so I returned to my unit to help tear down and pack away our tents and load equipment onto the deuce and a half trucks. Most tents were frozen solid a foot or more into the ground, Marines became frustrated breaking pics and axe handles while trying to free the tents from the ice. We worked at a grueling pace for hours barely make a dent in the ice, it was taking far longer to remove the tents from the ice than anyone expected. To free the tents we begin chopping off the bottom edges of the flaps, using pics, axes, and diesel fuel to free the edge of the tents from the ice covered rice patties. I was sick of this outdoor ice box and was ready to return to Okinawa where the weather was normal or at least felt normal.

After 12 weeks of taking only one scolding hot shower and sleeping on ice, I fantasize at the possibility of sleeping on a mattress and eating something else besides C-rations. Several days later we bordered a C-130 with our 105 cannons and half ton trucks shoved right in the middle of the air plane, we rode the entire trip with our knees shoved in our chess while holding our seabags on our lap. As uncomfortable as the ride was I was glad to be out of Korea and on my way back to Okinawa to a warmer climate. I couldn't help but to get lost in thoughts of Cindy and my new daughter. How fun it would be to be a father and the possibility of spoiling my daughter rotten.

I removed her picture from my pocket occasionally stared at it creating subliminal thoughts of spending time at the beach and park and celebrating her birthday. Thinking about my family made time pass quickly and before I knew it I was circling Okinawa looking across the vast wingspan of the C-130 airplane. It was a quick trubulent flight, we were toss around the the craft like rag dolls, our proped up on truck tires, miss directed heat from the plane engine burned our face as we grasped onto the nylon seating straps. We touch down several minutes later, shortly after landing we secured our gear, returned to formation, the first sergeant yelled liberty. Groups of ran through the showers like they were on fire, then down to the USO where the lines streched around the corner.

Marines yelled for honcho's (Cab) to whisk them two BC Street or Gate two known for legalize prostitution and seductive nightclubs. I didn't have interest in such things so I stay to myself, sat on my bed and envisioned being with my wife and my new baby girl. A month had past and I still found myself hanging around the base, playing bingo, and space invaders at the USO. I learned to eat with chopsticks, however the food was still foreign to me so I stuck with the simple dishes, large bowls of Ramen noodles or shrimp fried rice. That's how I visioned myself for the next nine months spending all of my time on base playing bingo, eating Ramen noodle and watching transformers in Japanese.

A week later I was approached by my body building roommate, he suggested showing me the layout and inter workings of the city. I was reluctant and callow, he was very bumptious and churlish, refusing to take no for an answer. I got dressed and off we went to BC Street in the back of a honcho. Jackson yelled, "Coco cing" that mean's Play Black music. The drived reached into his vase stack of tapes, a different tape for each race, before the first song was finished we arrived on one of the the most notorious streets on Okinawa. "BC street". Once our foot hit the pavement we walked at an infantry pace down the crowded military occupied streets of Okinawa Japan. Bars and clothing stores lined both sides of the street, paragon Asian woman strutted back and forth in front of the bars, touching, groping and caressing each soldier, sailor, Airman, or Marine that happen passed their door. We walk from bar to bar until we struck gold. A female stripper was about to perform a banana show, I was naïve to the night club culture but I was eager to watch and learn about this new culture but I soon discover this new culture would cost me at least two water down drinks. A pleasingly 6 foot tall demimonde Japanese stripper strutted out onto the ankle high stage. She concealed nothing. Her well constructed body was on display for all to see as she frolicked on the floor making love to a giant pillow, spreading her legs so I could visually conduct a pelvic exam.

I was unimpressed, although I had never been in a strip bar I thought it was bromidic and mundane. The Marines began to pound on the tables with fist, yelling "Banana show! Bananas show! Bananas show! Bananas show!" The stripper agreed to perform the banana show if everyone purchased another drink. We were all to eager to accommodate her meager wishes. I tried to get away with purchasing a Coke but I was forced to buy hard liquor if I want to stay for the show, so I ripped out a few dollars from my pocket and slap it on the table, ordering a rum and Coke. Most Marines in the club were only 20 years old are younger but it never bother the club owners they only wanted our US currency and didn't care about US Policies regarding age limits placed on drinking. Most of the merchants didn't want their own Yen they would rather have U.S dollars, so I didn't bother to the exchange my money for Japanese currency. I found the money system in Japan to be very strange, 1000 Yen equal $5 U.S dollars in 1980.

The strippers sashayed back and forth on the stage reminding me that I have been without a woman for three and a half months, so I sat anxiously waiting for the banana show to commence, slight drool leaked uncontrollably down the side of my mouth in a fountain of concupiscence. Suddenly she seductively pulled her see threw gown over her head tossing it on the floor for everyone to pass around the room and smell. She appeared lascivious at least we thought so, because she spread her legs wide-open and rubbed her breasts and thighs with coconut oil, she grab a banana and begin eroticizing it while slowly peeling away the skin. She licked the tip of the banana circularly at the top then began submerging the entire banana down her throat. We were all in a moment of prurient, moans and groans filter the room as young Marines creamed in their pants.

I clutched my glass of rum and coke nearly shattering the glass from the sultry sex act I just witness, but there was more to come. She laid her head back and slowly slid the banana inch by inch into her well stretched out bottomless pit of a vagina. You could have hear a pin drop as she slowly made the banana disappear into her deeply gorged out wound, then all of a sudden bananas fall sliced into perfect half inch pieces on a newspaper placed on the floor beneath her feet.

The slices were passed throughout the club and served on tooth picks as free appetizers for anyone who want more flavor in their drink. I like to get my freak on but I found this utterly disgusting so I took the party elsewhere. Jackson and I cruise the strip sticking our head's into different hotels and philandering the prostitutes behind the windows until we happened upon a hotel that had women that resemble models. Jackson quickly pulled out a wad of cash, tossing $15 to mama san and said "take your, pick I'm paying"

I said "no man I'm married" Jackson looked at me, he said "it's already paid for don't waste my money" then casually walked away leaving me standing there staring at 10 Asian beauties in the face. I couldn't resist I ask mamma san could she have them all stand up then I chose the tallest one. Mama san said.

"Go upstairs to the last room on the right side at the end of the hall."

Full of apprehension I slowly made my way down the poorly lit hallway. I slid open the door there was one twin size bed shoveled against the wall, the shower was 2 feet away with a water hose connected to the nozzle. I was totally naïve, I sat on the bed fully clothed, using up part of my 15 minutes. A minute later a slender graceful Asian female walked into the room and immediately begin stripping, her perky little nipples sprung out like flowers in the springtime.

I couldn't believe my eyes, her skin was as smooth as a manikin and her hair stretch down her back between the crack in her butt, she appear very at ease as she laid her slender beautiful body stretched across the bed. I froze like a deer in the headlights but she was unwilling to put up with my puerile behavior, she unzip my pants and put them down below my ankles, she reached up grab the collar of my shirt and pulled me crashing down on top of her small frame.

I couldn't believe it I was down and out in less than five minutes. She jumped up stepped into the shower and began washing with ice cold water from a water hose. I lay motionless on the bed smoking my mental cigarette, thinking about how good it was but how bad I felt inside. I stood there silently looking at her beautiful smooth skin and long dark soft hair scratching the bathroom floor hanging freely down her back.

I thought for second I could go again but she departed the room as quickly as she had enter. I didn't know what to think, this was definitely a vargary in my life. I didn't know whether to be happy or sad, knowing it was a common practice on the island to pay for sexual pleasure didn't make me feel any better because I have broken my sacred marital vows.

I resorted back to spending a majority of my time at the USO club, playing space invaders, watching TV and participating in occasional bingo games. Fortunate for me our next training exercise was less than a month away and before I knew it we packed up and shipped out to Mount Fuji Japan. This time on a US naval ship call the USS debuket. The birthing spaces were small and cramp, the metal bunkbeds were stacked five high with a rope supporting a piece of canvas used as the bed padding. The one man shower stall was very small, the toilets continually over ran spilling all over the bathroom floor due to the rocking of the ship.

This was my first time on a transporter ship and my first time feeling what it was like to be seasick, I layed on my cot for five days, eating only what the more experienced Marines brought me from the chow hall. I eat applesauce and drank water for the next five days. A couple more days had passed and I've grown less weary to the swaying and rocking of the ship. I was summoned by one Marine to follow him into the weld deck of the ship, I stuck my head out of the port and I couldn't believe my eyes, waves as tall as the buildings in downtown Indianapolis slammed unsympathetically against the bulkhead of the ship. It was as if we were being swallowed up by the ocean and never to be seen or heard from again. I've never seen something so powerful and overwhelming it made me realize how small and insignificant my life was and how powerful and forceful the earth is.

I lay in bed that night praying that we would arrive safely on the shores of Mount Fuji. I laid on my cot with my eyes wide open listening to the ship engine and propellers slowly whine and the powerful waves slam continuously against the side of the ship. I couldn't help but to think about Cindy in that moment, her meek but violent nature, just like the ocean she was calm until the plate Tech tonics in her mind change its course creating friction, causing her to erupt. I didn't know where I was going in this marriage but my first order of concerned is surviving while on this ocean.

The waves simmered so I made my way to the top deck, all I could see was endless waves of ocean as far as the eye could see, I never felt so small and insignificant and so out of place in the universe. I watch the ocean until I fall asleep with my back resting comfortably against a tire on a 105 howitzer. I was awakened four hours later by the coolness of the ocean mist on my face, and their she was, Mount Fuji, her summit peeking up towards the heavens and crested by the clouds more than 20 miles away.

I spent most of my life watching the tip of this mountain on TV and postcards, now it was right within my reach, upfront and personal. I couldn't believe it something I have fantasized about since I was eight years old while I watch Dean Martin and Jerry Lewis scary around Japan having fun. The moment of truth has arrived and I will be getting to know myself better then I have ever known myself before. Here we were arrogantly occupying another man's country, with rifles, cannons, helicopters, planes, and occupying force of 10,000 men.

We made an amphibious beach landing on the beaches, smoke billowing from the top of the tanks and Amtrak's as they plowed past the rugged shore line. Landing crafts were the main source used to land the infantry on the beach, others went to shore by helicopters and trucks. It was the most impressive sight. I've never seen so much armor and ships in my entire life. Ships lined up all the way out towards the break of the ocean and slowly disappeared into the fog.

Later that day we convoyed our way up the mountain to base camp, tanks, Amtrak's and trucks stretching from the shore of the beach to 10 miles in land. The base camp look like something straight out of 1950s

Marine Corps movie. Metal Quonset hut's in badly need of repair began at the edges of the nearest town angling up toward mount Fuji ending at the motor pool. We spent four months in mountain warfare training with Japanese soldiers who were located across the street. Unfortunately we didn't have any women at our base, neither did the Japanese. I don't think the Japanese soldiers mind not having women as much as the Americans did. Any spare time the Americans had we ventured out to nightclubs located downtown in Tokyo skyscrapers. The buildings contained nightclubs on each of the 25 floors.

There was a $25 admission that allowed us to go from floor to floor, stopping at each nightclub along the way. The native Asian girls were restless, they stood in line just to dance with us leaving their Japanese counterparts standing alone holding up the walls in envy. The young Japanese man appeared reluctant to express themselves freely because of their totalitarian Society. I didn't take comfort in the Japanese army base being across the street was, right where it was supposed to be far out in the middle of nowhere across the street from the Marine base. I couldn't imagine having a Japanese base across the street from the Marine Corps base in the United States, no other country will be able to set up shop and patrol neighborhoods throughout the United States without being attacked by its citizens. I thought it was very arrogant of the US and I knew deep down inside Japan hated having the US monitoring all their daily activities by foreign occupying forces. In retrospect the base was very small, situated right next to the well-known Mount Fuji volcano. Every morning for four months I stared up at the snowcapped mountain wondering when we were going to make our way to the top.

All the Marines knew the Marine Corps could not resist climbing a volcano, it was a small challenge but one we would have to face before leaving the island. The ground was covered with broken up pieces of lava on a concave slope. The motor pool, and gun park was placed at the highest point on the base directly in front of the volcano. The base look very barren, old and run down, there wasn't a woman within miles of the base, Takahara was the closest town to the base, approximately 2 miles away, the perfect walking distance for a fit marine.

There was nothing on this base except for Marines. The recreation department try to entertain us by showing old movies in an empty shack and giving us discounted blue ribbon beer. What they couldn't sell they give away for free at the end of the night. Old cable sproles were use for tables which turn out to be a good choice because Marines fought every night over things that wouldn't makes sense to the average civilian. After having a few beers someone would we get liquor courage, stand up and yell out "Artillery!", another marine would yell out "Amtrak's"! And another would yell out "infantry!" Before I knew it there was a full fledged fight taking place. I punch my way to the door and out the back exit before the MP'S arrived.

The next morning Marines were line up at the chow hall bandaged from head to toe. The commanding officers didn't seem to mind, they were raking in plenty of money, at the din of inquity, therefore; they decided to let the club continued to operate for the next several months. Every night for four months there was a fight, I stayed in the club long enough for the first bowl of peanuts to be thrown then I left before the full fight could escalate involving more then 30 young Marines. There was just another form of entertainment, we had nothing to do but drink liquor, eat Ramen noodle, and beat each other senseless. I spend my weekends with two Jarhead friends trying to learn the city and figure out how to catch the bullet train to Tokyo.

We got fed up with hanging around the base and fighting in the night clubs so we got dressed one night and ventured out to the train station in Takahara. We couldn't read the signs, everything was in Japanese, not a single word in English. Unlike the US, Japan wasn't as politically correct as the United States. They're only concern was with their native people and language, no other language can be found anywhere in the city, but we were desperate, so we paid our money and boarded the train hoping to land somewhere near Tokyo. Four hours passed by and we were still in the middle of nowhere, all we could see from the train window was farm land and Rice patties as far as the eye can see. We rode from sun up to sundown and never reached anything that resembled a city. We got off the train several stops at different stations wondering around like Tourist from another country lost in the US, by this time we come to realize the only way we were go to find Tokyo was if Godzilla were to appear and started chasing Japanese all over the place leading us to downtown Tokyo.

At least seven hours had passed and I was no longer interested in going to Tokyo I just want to return to the base because I was starving at this point, even a box of C-rations sound edible. One Japanese citizens couldn't help but to noticed how confused and lost we looked. He offered to help us find our way back on the right course to Takahara if he could practice using his English on us. We were more than glad to oblige him. He spoke English and we complemented his language skills and praised him on everything he said, although we could barely understand anything he said. We wanted to make him feel comfortable enough to ride four hours back to Mount Fuji with us. He was a very nice and pleasant man, it appear that he had just gotten off work heading home with a newspaper tucked under his arms and decided to help a fellow man in need. I thought it was the most thoughtful jester I had ever witnessed.

The other two Marines were flabbergasted by his annoying non-stop talking and the way he pronounce his words, abusing the English language, so they called it a night and passed out on the benches of the train. I tried to be grateful and listen as he talked, nodding my head occasionally as if I was actively listening. I was so focused on getting back to the base I Harley noticed the beautiful Japanese ladies standing shoulder to shoulder less then a foot away. The train slowly pulled into the takahara station, we gratefully shook the strangers hand, waved goodbye and began our journey back to the base. It was pitch black dark like the desert, we could only see 3 feet in front of us, fortunately a Japanese soldier happened by.

"Where are you going" he asked,

"We're on our way back to the Marine Corps base" "This way "he said".

I was shocked by the continued kindness with everyone I encountered at Mount Fuji, each of them went out-of-their-way to ensure that we were okay. I was confused I thought they would have hated us for occupying their land and forcing our will and the American way upon them, but they were kind and very humble. The train station was only a 20 minute walk from the base the Japanese soldier walk beside us and begin asking us if we would like to sell our high school rings or if he could buy porn magazine from us.

He reached into his cargo pockets and pulled out a Japanese porn magazine. I flipped through the pages, all the women were stretched out with their legs wide open but there was one small problem, they were wearing panties, only exposing their breast. I immediately understood why he wanted American pornographic magazines, our women weren't so modest, you can see right into their birth canal if you looked in the right magazine. We didn't sell any high school rings that night or give away any American porn magazines. We waved goodbye as we turned left and he turned right back into our military commands.

The next day I couldn't help but to make my way back out to Town once more but not before stopping and getting a one dollar succulent juicy burrito loaded with unidentifiable meat.

I heartedly chow down on the burrito while walking towards the front gate. Halfway into the burrito I bit something hard. I reached in my mouth and pulled out a huge canine tooth. I thought nothing of it and tossed it to the side and continue chowing down. I didn't venture far from the front gate just far enough to browse through a few stores, meet a few of the towns people then back into the gate I went. Later that day I was informed I would be standing guard duty for the next 15 to 20 days, I didn't mine because my unit was schedule to go on a 15 to 30 mile hike with the infantry division every Friday before securing for the day.

I stood at the armory and watch my unit leave every Friday morning at 5 AM with full gear including backpacks, helmets, rifles, flack Jackets, 60 Calibar and 50 Calibar machine guns. I wanted no part of it. They were gone all day until five in the evening, returning with blisters on their feet barley able to walk. Somehow I believe the Marine Corps use this as a device to slow the young Marines down and tire them out before letting them go on liberty. Although the guard shifts were four hours on and four hours off I didn't mine, even when it rained. I would just walk to the back of the armory and stood beneath the shelter we Jerry rigged just for that purpose. 2 AM in the morning Hunger would set in, there was no shortage of food because C-Rations for the entire battalion was stored at the armory. All I had to do was pull a case of C-Rations from the stack and take what I wanted out-of-the-box, this was called rat fucking the C-Rations.

The rain poured down unforgivably as I stood under the tarp. I used my can opener called a John Wayne for cutting holes in the bottom of a C-Ractions can to make a stove. I shivered uncontrollably from my soaked camouflage utilities and my saturated leather boots. I couldn't believe how cold it was turning, I was hoping we would return to Okinawa before winter weather hit the island.

I had just come from Korea and I wasn't mentally or physically ready to freeze to death anytime soon. The top of the volcano already had a snow capped and it was rumored that we were climbing the volcano within a weeks. Just as I was feeling sorry for myself I heard a banging sound coming from one of the canisters, I reached down into my ammo pouch and remove three 12 gauge shells. I loaded my pump shotgun, cocking it, placing one Shell in the chamber. I creeped toward the banging noise, slowly I squatted down and peaked around the corner. A hooded man was pounding away trying to break the lock on the canister that house more than 300 weapons.

"Halt" I yelled as I stood up.

The would-be thief threw the crowbar at me hitting the cocking mechanism of my shotgun, defensively I let go of a burst barely catching the would-be thief on the side of her face knocking him to the ground, the pumping action on my shotgun had been damaged just enough to prevent me from housing another shell, so I rushed the thief and smashed him in the face with the butt of my weapon.

"Halt" I said once again while pressing the borrow of my disabled shotgun into the side of his face. Within seconds the reactionary team surrounded us and took the thief into custody.

I loved guard duty it got me out of shit details throughout the day, I was no longer the guy to call when the head needs to be scrubbed down or when the shitter's need to be burnt. I spent my mornings hanging around the barracks, cleaning my cameras and writing letters home. Cindy often occupied the blank thoughts in my mind during idle moments. I couldn't help but think of her and the mistake I made joining the military. She was always on my mind even at night as I cried in my sleep thinking about her and my daughter. I didn't know this will be a common theme of my life every time we were apart.

The nights were cold and silent with the exception of the enlisted men's club, where fights broke out continuously throughout the night. One night I was lying soundly asleep in my rack, the lights flickered on then the reactionary alarm sounded. My guard unit was summonsed to the club to break up a fight, we surrounded the building with nightsticks in hand, one white man ran out of the club yelling and screaming pointing in my direction and yelling nigger! at the top of his lungs. All the sudden there I was staring into the twisted face of hate, I live my entire young life in Indianapolis and only in America do I have to travel 12,000 miles across the ocean, to Japan to be called a nigger by an American Marine.

I wasn't phased at all by his uneducated remark, I simply tossed him on the ground and cuffed has hands behind his back, making sure he didn't break free I squeeze the handcuffs extra tight, then I locked them in place with my handcuff key. I stood guard for another 10 days before returning to my unit Just in time to go on a 24.3 mile hike with full gear. We were packed up and ready to move out at 4 AM in the morning, the torrential rain was coming down hard in golf ball size droplets that morning. The base was flooded within two minutes of the first rain fall, letting up for two minutes at the most. We held off the march as long as we could but there was no signs of the rain letting up so we headed out with 50 pounds of gear, 50 caliber machine guns, 60 caliber machine gun, mortars and mortar plates and tubes. We slipped and slid up-and- down the mountains and Slippery roads, one Marine took the time to turn around and snap my picture as we came to the end of our hike.

We ran up and down around the mountains at an infantry pace, if I didn't know better I thought this hike wasn't going to end. Five hours into the hike I begin to feel blisters forming on my soaking wet feet. Temperatures begin to drop as we approach the end of the fall season moving towards the winter. The ground became a little harder and colder and the rain felt like ice water hitting our bodies. I didn't know what hurt most, my feet or the edges of my ears. My camouflage utilities and flak jacket we're so saturated they felt like 50 pounds of wet sand. 15 miles into the hike the signal was given for my battery to move to the head of formation.

That meant we had to run 2 miles past the platoons while they stood on the side of the road cheering us on as we ran in Formation through the entire battalion. Water slashing beneath our boots while dragging the machine guns to the top of mountain. Finally the end was insight. I could see the antiquated barracks as we toppled the rise of the mountain, but the barracks were still at least 3 miles away. One of the commanders got motivated and decided we're going to run the last 3 miles and off we went Machine guns and all. We came to a halt in the front of are Quonset huts, I was so exhausted and dehydrated my eyelids felt as if there were glued to the top of my head. After we put away our gear we were dismissed for the evening, although our feet were blistered and we were exhausted the entire battalion headed for the showers all it once, everyone scurried into the shower trying to wash up before going to town. We still used the system of showering we learned in Boot Camp. One man jump in the shower and get wet then jumps out and soaps Down, while the other Man is getting wet. Then the man jumps in the shower rinses off the soap while the other Man soaps down. It was a very systematic universal method of expedience showering.

 The showers ran constantly until everyone was done, the water on the floor was at least ankle high if not higher, everyone was required to wear shower shoes but scum and razor blades floated freely in the water. A clean up crew was made up by the non-hackers, anyone who dropped out or fail back on the 24.3 mile hike. I was glad I was in top physical condition but due to the scum floating above the water it would be the first time in my life I would contract athletes feet. My feet were blistered from front to back and there was still rumors that we will be climbing Mount Fuji the next coming week.

 Most Marines got dressed and headed to Tokyo, I stayed around the base writing letters to my wife and playing basketball with two of my good friends. After an exhausting day of climbing Mount Fuji we were boarding ships and on our way back to Okinawa, two day's into the trip a typhoon struck right in the middle of the pacfic ocean, waves as tll as the building in downtown Indianapolis. The waves came crashing down, slamming on top of our canons and weapons lockers. Porpoises swim at an infantry pace along side the ship appearing to be un affected by the large waves.

 The ship engines hummed and wind through the trublent storm, climing wave after wave for more than five hours but, the captian didn't want to risk capsizing the ship, therefore; we were force to pull into a naval port in Yokohama Japan. We were reluctantly stuck in Yokohama Japan for three days until the typhoon resided. The young Marines took advantage of the military base and PX, stocking up on food to take back to the ship for the two-week ride home. I spend my time at teh base running back and forth to 31 flavors ice cream and a Japanese barbecue restaurant. Unfortunate for myself I was constipated, I hadn't taken a dump in 14 days. Due to the lack of proper dietary meals provided by the Marine Corps I was destined to report to sick bay.

The C-rations did exactly as they were designed to do, I sat on the toilet for hours while the boat rocked back-and-forth splashing the toilet water all over my buttockc, forcing me to call it quits and visit sick- bay. The corpsman said I was constipated and he needed to give me an enema. I thought it was something to eat like a chocolate candy bar. Smelling from ear to ear I stuck my hand out and said "give it here"

The corpsman said, "No you have to get undressed" My eyes grow wide open.

"Just to eat a piece of chocolate?" I said.

He went to his medicine cabinet and remove a plastic bottle with a long stem.

"I will have to fill this with a solution", then you'll lay on your side while I put this tube in your anus and squeeze the liquid from the bottle into your rectum.

Apprehensively I begin pulling down my pants, suddenly I stop and reverse my pants in the oppsite direction, pulling my pants up.

I said. "I'm feeling a little better now, I think I can use the bathroom without your help, thanks anyway."

Out of no-where two Gay sailor's appeared blocking the door. I knew I could run right through them but the ranking seaman pulled rank.

"We can't let you leave, we must perform the procedure". He said.

"But I'm feeling okay I don't need a procedure" I said, while backing up towards the door.

The two corpsmen stood in the room watching, smiling and giggling to themselves. I thought to myself.

"When I get a chance I'm going to throw both of these assholes overboard. However, I had no choice, so I laid on the table and turn on my side allowing the corpsmen to perform this procedure. It was a valuable lesson learned, the next time I had this problem, I would keep my mouth shut and waited it out.

By the time I return to the Okinawa I only had one month left on the island. I spent most of my time hanging around the base and trying not to get myself into anymore quagmires or promiscuous situations. I couldn't believe it January 5, 1981, I was on my way back to Indianapolis, I could burley sit still on the plane. I tried to fall asleep to hurry time alone. I fell asleep for four hours when I woke up I still had 10 hours to go before I even reached Alaska, I counted every hour, every minute and every second until I touchdown in Indianapolis. I walked in the door of Cindy's mothers house and their she was in the middle of the room trying too peek over-the-top of her play pen. She was so pretty with her hair resting on top of her head and a pretty little face any dad would love.

I scooped her up into my arms and it was as if she knew who I was the whole time, we immediately bonded, wherever I went she went with me and for a brief second I forgot all about Okinawa Japan and the shame I brought to my marriage.

Later that evening Cindy and I laid in bed staring at one another, trying to firgure out what the other person was thinking about. Michaela set between us sucking up all the attention as her nine month brain could stand. At one moment our eyes locked and I could see the wheels spinning in Cindy's mind, she looked at me with a question mark on her face and I look back at her as though I knew the answer to whatever questions she wanted to ask. She dared not asked the fatal question, "If I had been faithful to her while overseas." She just rolled over onto her side and rub Michaela's back trying to get her to fall asleep. The sun flickr one last time then closed it's eyes as it set down behind the sky scraping buildings for the night. Cindy laid on her side wearing a very reviling pink night gown, I stared at her back inching closer and closer until we were lock in the human pretzel position. My mind ran wild thinking about her intimately making love with another man. The thought of her plausible disloyalty was lodged in my murky subconscious, opening an opportunity to reflect on my own disgruntled behavior. I couldn't deny it and I didn't want to admit it, so I just laid there as if I never heard a word.

The next 29 days would be more of the same, I felt the boundaries of our marriage had been breached at both ends of the spectrum and no one was innocent. Three weeks later my orders stated I was to return to Camp Pendleton and report for duty. My family will arrive at the base within two months, so my first order of business was to buy a car. The artillery base camp was more than 14 miles away from base housing. Although the city bus was walking distance from my front door I wanted the luxury of leaving the house at the last minute and not having to leave two hours early just to catch two city buses and one military bus before reaching my barracks.

One evening I decided to leave the base and cruise Oceanside boulevard in search of a dependable car. After visiting several car lots I determine all the car lots were selling junk, the best car lot was out of my reach, located in San Diego, so I reluctantly purchased a 1972, Lavender blue Cadillac El Dorado. Even a laymen like myself knew it was a piece of junk. The car had no problem leaving me stranded on desolate parts of the base, the first week the engine caught fire, a month later the transmission went out, the horn didn't work and the gas guzzling piece of junk only got 12 miles a gallon. I couldn't have picked a worse car if I put my name in a drawing for it. People seem to be impressed that I was driving a Cadillac and often question whether the car was mine. The car rode smooth as if it were riding on clouds, but sat on pins and needles wait for the next break down.

Cindy arrived right on schedule two months later, I wasted no time preparing the house, making it livable and comfortable. We didn't have many friends, therefore; we just occasionally walk to the beach or take trips to the mall. I was excited for Cindy to experience California, it will be her first time traveling this distance from home, therefore; I knew I had to make personal adjustments, making sure she was comfortable, but those adjustments would be invein.

Sometimes, doing the quiet hours of the night when Michaela was in bed sleep, Cindy would lay on the front room floor and talk about missing her brother, as tears stream down her face I didn't know what to do, I had little experince in the arears of counseling and with the help of the Corps I was emotionally bankrupt, so I just listen, once in a while I would try to redirect her thoughts toward other things. Later that month came the news, she was pregnant again, I wasn't surprised since we just came off of a 30 day sex benj. My time in the U.S. Marine Corps ws coming to an end. I had less then 24 months left in the Corps, I had to start making plans for the near future because I will be getting discharged soon.

Cindy didn't care for the military life, she never got use to me being gone for extended periods of time. I did understand her reasoning so

PEACE TIME MARINES

I offer to send her back to Indianapolis for 12 weeks are until she was ready to return. In two months she was on a plane back to Indianapolis and I was on a 5 ton truck heading to 29 Palms California for 12 weeks of desert training.

The training was gruesome, and dirty. The sand stung my skin like bits of broken glass. There wasn't many places to take cover from the sun beating down mercilessly on us, not giving us much of a break doing the waking hours. During night training, the sky was lit up for miles, covered with illumination shells floating in the sky long enough to light a target area more than a mile long or at least several grid squares. Before the illumination flickr out we unleashed over 1000 artillery, tanks. Mortars, and aircraft shells across a mile long stretch of desert. Tanks set 100 m in front of our cannons, dug deep into ditches, they would roll up on top of the ditch long enough to pump out one shell then back down in the ditch they would go. Helicopters were next, they would fly in and shoot up the area with 1000 rounds then spin off Just in time for the low flying jets to drop a quick 500 pound white phosphorus bomb in the target area, next artillery pumped out five shells from each canon simultaneously firing a 50 Cal machine gun from the top of the trucks.

We repeated this operation over and over again until we had it perfect. We call this the iron curtain. This was a last ditch effort when all at else has failed and the enemy seemed unstoppable. The constant firing drove the Canon spades deep into the ground, I knew we were set in for the night not making another long dreaded road trip to the next position or so I thought, until someone yelled out the word "CSM0" that meant to pack your gear and move out quickly. Everyone began slinging artillery shells, shovels, pics, and axis onto the back of the 5 ton truck. Tanks came out of nowhere as though they were hidden in the ground, smoke billowing from their stack, helicopters hovering above escorting us to our next position, while jets buzz the ground leaving trails of CS gas and the young marines scrambling to don their gas mask and cover themselves with their ponchos.

The CS gas burned our eyes causing us to choke and vomit as we hurried to displace our weapons, the sun flickered one last time before it hide its fiery face behind the concave slopes of the sand covered mountains. Everyone was lined up on the road ready to move onto the next position, the trucks were loaded up form floor to teh roof with loose gear and unspent shells.

The spades of my cannon were stuck deep in the sand. This was quite the conundrum, all the other trucks were lined up on the role and slowly pulling off. We had to dig out a spot beneath the trail of the Canon and place a jack under the trail of the Canon and dreacinate the spade far enough out of the ground to allow us to move the canon trail slightly toward a closing position. After 20 minutes of furiously digging out the space of my Canon we got the cannon hooked up to the truck. I looked up and my unit was gone as well as the sun. I broke out my Night vision goggles, map, compass and combat flashlight then navigated my way to our new firing position.

At one point during the drive I thought for sure we were lost, It seemed as if we had been driving all night into the morning. I didn't see my unit for hours, but I knew how to effectively read a map and use a compass. Finally arriving at the new position only minutes behind my unit, everyone was so exhausted from the long drive and the late hours, no one seemed to notice that I was not in the proper truck line order.

We repetitiously emplaced and displaced the Canon several times throughout the night, by the time I had a chance to look at my watch it was close to 2 am in the morning, everyone was just concerned with getting their cannons in position for the next artillery barrage. The entire firing line was quiet and pitch black dark and all of a sudden at 3 AM in the morning some young private got the urge to make coffee. The inexperience marine lit a heat tap which illuminated the entire gun line. You can see the men walking around the cannons from a mile away.

A dust storm with feet scurried across the desert yelling and screaming while walking at an infantry pace. Gunnery Sgt. Jef-fords came yelling down the gun line "who the hell lit that fire'? "put it out god damnit, put it out". He said, while walking at an infantry pace with his hands shoved deep in his pockets and the light of the Moon refracting brilliantly off of his bald head. It was freezing in the desert and at this time we were on our third day of training with no sleep, everyone was on edge, we were a bunch of walking time bombs waiting to explode. Our physical condition and stamina was being tested in every sense, heat exhaustion in the afternoon and freezing half to death at night. I just about had enough of the Desert and the military training, the wind was beginning to kick up again, my goggles couldn't prevent the sand from edging its way into my eyes. By the time reveille was sound my eyes were woefully swollen shut. I made my way to sick bay located in the back of a supplies truck, not before emptying two canteens of water on my face loosening the sand that scratched the cornea of my eye.

The Navy corpsmen only care about getting to the chow truck early in the morning so he just poured water on my eyelids and told me to report back to my unit. I pride my eyes lids open with my fingers, once I cleaned the sand from the corner of my eyes I was able to see well enough to set the deflection and quadrant on the Canon sight for the next fire Mission.

Once again the sand kicked up like a small tornado but this time it was due to the helicopters that came out of the sky like locus and landed 50 feet from my firing position. I was ordered to push the cannon into the back of the helicopter and carry one case of artillery shells. Off we went flying to another desolate place in the desert to conduct what we called a hip shoot. Once the helicopter landed, we push the cannon down the metal ramp out of the rear of the helicopter at an exaggerated pace. The two marines in the front of the cannon controlled the breaks, both men had to be experts with breaking, if the breaks were put in place to quick or hard the spades would hit the helicopter blades causing an explosion, killing everyone on the copter. After successfully extracting from the copter I shot a quick asthma with my compass, pointed the cannon in the designated direction then we pumped out two artillery shellsdown range, then back on the helicopter as quick as we landed.

This was called internal raids, because the canon was placed inside the helicopter rather than being towed from the bottom of the helicopter. We landed back in our staging area, connected the Canon back onto the truck and off we went down the road to our next firing position. I was starving so I dug into my cargo pocket and pulled out a piece of Poggie bait. I ripped a piece of jerky apart with my teeth and chewed on it to get some type of nutrition. I could barley eat while the truck raced down the desert road at 50 miles an hour, tossing artillery shells around in the back of the truck while the man got swallowed up by the desert sand.

It was a tremendously fast pace and very early in the morning, it was barley 4:00 AM and I hadn't had breakfast, I hadn't got a shave, nor have I taken a dump. We continued at this pace for the next 12 weeks. I was truly physically and mentally beat up and drained, at the time I didn't believe anything in my life could have matched what I was going through at this time. The more training I had the further remove I was from Society. I didn't think I could ever be a civilian again, I can only exist in the civilian world in a physical state but my true heart and experiences and life lessons would come from what I experienced in the Corp.

After 12 weeks of eating nothing but C-rations my digestive system was permanently damaged. I haven't taken a dump in 8 days. Subliminal thoughts flashed before my eyes of having decent meal. There I was in the middle of the desert visioning an oasis of regular food, even the food from the chow hall seen appetizing to me at this point, if the planets lined up and the sun moved into it's fifth solar house, the promise of pantheism would see fit to give us one hot meal from the main base. But that was wishful thinking, C-rations was the only meal we would see until the end of this training exercise, because C-rations were designed to clog our system making us constipated so that we couldn't interrupt our work by running to the bathroom once a day.

This gave us more time to focus on our job. It took most of us 12 minutes to take a dump so the order of the day was too carry a stack of newspapers or magazines to provide a form of distraction while we pinched a loaf and focus on something other than the pain while cleansing our colon. The portable toilet was crafted out of an ammunition box with layers of duct tape used for padding the seat. It was a hard way to live and I promised I would encourage any young person to go else where, the Marines weren't the place to be, living in dirt and squalor, sleeping one hour and working 18 hours a day was the norm during training.

This life was certainly not for the weak at heart and for the moment I didn't think it was me. I had approximately 13 months left in the corp and I lost plenty of sleep thinking about the possibility of becoming a civilian. Working a 9 to 5, no NCO duty, no field ops, and no unit rotations or oversee deployments. I was ready for the real world and for the civilian minded attitude that will came with it. The Marines have made me into a very punctual and dependable person, it would be a hard adjustment to be around people who just cruise through their day. The Marines function on high-energy and fast-paced, slowing down to a civilian pace would be mental torture. I didn't have any idea of how to be a civilian again but I was willing to give it a try even if that meant I will lose some of my military bearing. I was ready to try something different, something that didn't require me to polish my shoes or press my uniform. I was thoroughly tired of the bullshit and ready to resume my life as a civilian, with a civilian job, and civilian ideas.

THE ME NOBODY KNOWS

After 12 rugged weeks of dragging our cannons behind half ton trucks in the dusty sands of 29 palms, we packed up and headed back to Camp Pendleton, so we thought'. Right before Our convoy was rerouted to the San Diego Pier we received two new privates fresh out of Boot Camp. We boarded a troop transporter ship heading overseas. Private Dunbar one of the new privates was assigned to my section. He was kind of a goofy kid and if a strong wind came along it will blow his 110 pound body right over. I didn't think much of him and my presumptions were right. He immediately began to get into mischief and I found myself standing in front of the captains door explaining why I didn't have control of him.

I had to manually resolve this issue, therefore; I placed him on every shit detail that came down the pike. It was time to depart and as the ship slowly back away from the port the entire battalion stood on the deck of the ship while being dragged out to sea by two tug boats. Dunbar stood next to me practically leaning against me as the wind blew violently across the deck of the ship loosening some of our cargo straps.

I didn't know where we were going nor did I bother to ask, once aboard the ship I settled into my birthing area and sack down for the night. I stayed in the bed during most of our two-week trip except during the times we held formation or when I had to stand guard duty. I found the ship to be very peaceful, the quietness in the night gave me a chance to think clearly about what I would do after I was discharged from the Marine Corps. Sometimes I would set on the top deck from sunrise to sunset watching the ocean and the porpoise swimming along side the ship. After about a month of floating around aimlessly on the ocean a small rise of land appeared out of nowhere, I could hear the captain of the ship talking to my Company commander.

"That's our next objective." He said, pointing to the barren land.

I started preparing my section by taking an ammo Count and ensuring that we had Night vision goggles and binoculars. I sent private Dunbar to the armory to secure two pairs of night vision goggles, he took the Liberty to tell the armory sergeant he was promoted to squad leader and was to be issued a .45 caliber pistol with four magazines along with several pouches of ammunition. Dunbar returned to the squad equipped with two pairs of night vision goggles, smelling from area ear to ear as though he had just won the lottery, with his .45 caliber pistol tucked safely out of view he became mysteriously quiet and off to himself. I was rather pleased and thought I have broken him from his bad habits and childlike behavior, so I left him to himself until it was time to board the landing craft.

Three hours later we were shoved into a landing craft, and once again the onslaught of ocean water spilling uncontrollably inside the craft. I was hoping it wasn't another training exercise where they made us jump out of the landing craft and swim ashore, but this couldn't be a training exercise because we were carrying full clips of ammo. After wandering aimlessly around the ocean for several hours we begin our journey towards the shore, the landing craft went up and down the shore trying to bypass the coral reef but we had no such fortune. They had to let us out about 100 yards from the beach. The door fell and the Ocean water rushed right inside the landing craft soaking us up to our knees. From the back of the landing craft I got a running start and jump 3 feet out into the Ocean, I Kick my way a shore pulling private Dunbar and one other marine right along with me, whom were struggling to stay afloat because of the heaviness of their camouflage Utilities and flak jacket.

After reaching the staging area we quickly divided our sections into two squads, this time we didn't have our cannons, we became instant infantrymen gearing up to head out on a recon mission. We were divided into two small nine man squads . We quickly wipe the salty ocean water off our M-16s, just as my M-16 was wiped down and oil, it was snatched from my hands and replaced with a 12 gauge pump shotgun.

"Gray take this compass and map, you're on point," the staff sergeant said.

I only had 13 months left in the suck and I wasn't trying to get killed with a little more than a year left in the Corp. I couldn't help but to ask.

"Why am I on point, this job is reserved for a private, not an NCO!". I said.

"We need someone that knows how to competently use a compass and read a map". The staff sergeant said.

I loaded five shells in my shotgun, orientated my map and shot an asthma towards the designation.

We formed a line on each side of the road, being in artillery it was natural we'd would ride a portion of the way but instead we humped on foot like the infantry. The American arrogance was upfront and in-your-face, we were in Country less than 12 hours and we walked around like we own the place. The sun fell down behind the landscape before we could walk our first 20 miles, It was instantly dark. I couldn't see 2 feet in front of my face. The marines behind me watch the reflectors on the back of my helmet ahrdly reflecting off the moon light, every time I stopped, both squads would stop then moved to the side of the road and kneel down until I started moving again. We must've walked for hours, the dry air and smoldering heat waves made my mouth dry like cotton but, we were forbidden to drink from our canteens to prevent water from splashing around. We stop for a minute and set up on the side of the road, they said there was troop movement coming our way, a small group of about 15 soldiers, so we position ourselves to set an ambush.

Two hours went by and still there were no soldiers. In the meantime Dunbar laid at the rear of the squad off to the side of the road caught up in his in his own world. He removed his new toy from his waistband and began playing with and polishing his new .45 caliber pistol. Loading and unloading it unbeknownst to the rest of the squad. Suddenly a group of undisciplined Lebanese soldiers were patrolling, they were heading directly toward our position. I signal for both squads to standby. The moment intensified with each annonying step boots. I was so nervous, every step they took echo like big drums pounding in my ear. I could hear myself breathing heavily the closer they got. I slowly began to get into a kneeling position, rotating the butt of the weapon into my shoulder and positioning my finger to squeeze off the first shut.

Just as I was applying pressure to the trigger, an unauthorized shot was fired from no-where making the soldiers turned and ran the other way. Dunbar had accidentally discharged his unauthorized .45 caliber weapon. My first response was to send him to the rear and placed him on a shit detail until we return to the rear and process him for NJP 'nonjudicial punishment'. But that didn't happen, because we were too far out into the sticks, to far from the closest town and there was no turning back at this point so we were forced to allow him to continue on with us. We walked four more hours before the rock in my boot began bruising my foot.

I was just about growing tired and weary of playing Marine when all of a sudden I bumped into someone coming from the opposite direction. We stood facing one another for what seemed like an hour but it was less than 15 seconds. I didn't know how who he was or whether he was friendly of allie,. The only thing I did know for sure, I didn't want to die nor did I want to kill another person. I couldn't see him and he couldn't see me. I know all the friendly's were were behind me, and not coming from the other direction. We stood so close I could feel his breath, his clothing smelled of burnt wood. It was so quiet I could hear his heart rapidly beating.

My palms were dripping with sweat, I was gripping my shot gun so tight I accidentally force the cocking lever forward, the shotgun made a clicking noise in the echoing atmosphere of the night so loud it could be heard from a mile away.

"I was in it now" I thought to myself.

I felt his arm make a slight shift and before he could complete his motion I leveled my shot gun pulling the cocking mechanism home letting go of one shell. Everyone scattered to the side of the road, the silence was palpable, my heart was racing 100 miles an hour as I lay silently in the ditch trying to slow down my breathing, but nothing helped. I thought for sure there would be more of them and a all out gun battle would ensue. No one spoke a word, everyone lay silently in the dirt until the next morning. The sun rose slowly that morning as we all merged onto the road to witness what was no surprise from the night before. A young soldier laid alone, spread Eagle on the road, half his face and hand blown off. I thought it ironic, I hated the arrogance of American but I got the first American kill. Everyone thought it was cool that I killed someone, I was bona fide.

"The first kill of the day they said", "You're going to get a medal for this one!" one private yelled, as they all took souvenirs from the young soldier's body. I stood there staring at the body, I didn't have time to process what happened before I was summons to the rear of the squad.

One Marine broke his leg jumping in the ditch, he was being medevac back to the ship so I reluctantly swap my 12 gauge shotgun in exchange for his M 16 rifle then returned to my position as point man. Within the hour we were walking over the ridge into a small village, the war between Israel and the PLO have not yet started but it appear that all the buildings in the Village were practically burned to the ground. We broke into two squads of nine and enter the Village from two different directions, to prevent crossfire the first squad moved towards the South entrance of the village, my squad headed in from the West.

Stuck in the point position I was the first man into the building, I wasn't worried about the possibility of occupants because the buildings were supposed to be empty, but from the looks of the town no one could possibly exist in such a barren and burnt out place. The first building had holes blown in the wall large enough to walk through with ease. I stuck my head through the hole in wall, not from fear of an attack but bacause the building was barley standing, without being too temerity I judiciously made my way up the steps, one of the privates tap me on the back of my leg indicating that he heard a noise coming from outside, being a de facto leader I sent two Marines to check the noise then preceded up the steps.

As I turned to look up the staircase a grenade was tossed over the balcony, striking me on front of my face then rolling under the staircase and exploding. I fell uncontrollably from the second flight of the stairs, hitting the concrete floor losing my helmet and almost shattering my knee. The hand guards on my M-16 shattered into pieces as I hit the concrete. Unexpectedly another small explosion went off just big enough to knock me crumbling back to the floor. Before I could get my focus someone grabbed me by the collar of my flack Jacket and begin dragging me out of the building, across the street to another building and threw me down a flight of stairs into a basement.

"What the fuck" I thought.

As I struggle to get to my feet, I was struck in the face with the butt of a rifle, I was struck once more before blood started trickling down my face blurring my vision, I laid very still on the floor pretending I was helpless and unconscious.

I stuck my bruised hand under my T-shirt graspings my palm size combat knife, I listen attentively for how many soldiers were in the room, one soldier walked over and placed his foot on my head, he raise his machete high in the air, before he could strike, the wall exploded, giving me time to spin around and shove my knife into his thigh. I twisted the knife into his leg and pulled out a chunk of flesh, suddenly his head disintegrated into small chunks of flesh, he was shot several times in the face. It was Dunbar, he unloaded an entire m-16 magazine into the soldiers face, within minutes the room was filled with the first squad. Helicopter transporters were called in and I was medevac back to the ship, I wasn't hurt, I just had scratches and cuts here and their but I was glad to be out of that desolate place and back aboard the comforts of the Navy ship. Our Recon mission was successful, we provided solid evidence that the enemy materiel have been occupying the town for sometime.

I sat on the top deck of the ship and read my novel "The King of torts". Later that day Dunbar was locked away in the ships Brig for his own safety and ours. Later in the month he was given an other than honorable discharge. I was so disenchanted by the smal conflict, I harley notice rockets fired back-and-forth across the vast wasteland. In two weeks time the islands slowly disappear as we set sail out to sea as another group of carriers arrived. We were relieved and rotated back to the states. The ocean was angry once again, slapping its waves harshly against the ships bulkhead.

I didn't mind the slamming of the waves this time, it seem to provide a calming effect from the shotgun blast ringing in my subconscious, the rifle butt to the face, the exploding walls and the falling pieces of facial flash. I sat on the top deck of the ship wishing I was somewhere else. From a distance I can see my luminary platoon sergeant walking at an infantry pace in my direction. I could tell he was purpose driven, assigning guard duty to anyone enjoying the view on the top deck, it was no suprise, the minute you tried to relax the oldlong time tradition of harassment was one of the joys we all suffer in the corp. He walked towards me at an infantry pace scribing as he walked with a menacing look on his face staring me in my direction. He stepped next to me, bent over bonhomie touching on the shoulder, then he walked over to another marine assigning him to guard duty. I guess he could see I've been through enough in the last few days, so he was magnanimous and avuncular at a time I needed space and clarity of thought.

Although it really didn't matter whether I stood guard duty or not, I would've stayed on top deck and off to myself, but I was appreciative of his kind gesture. For the next week I sat in the weld deck of the bottom of the ship, I climbed into the back of one of the deuce and a half trucks, where I could get a good night of uninterrupted sleep, and no one would hear me crying in my sleep. Everyone seemed to be having a good time, drinking beer, eating lobster and steak, celebrating our last week on the ship. I was suffering a guilty conscious of my American sin. I knew that sins pay wages, even though I was following orders it didn't abdicate me from the responsibility of taking another human life. I secluded myself from others, staying in the back of the truck for the next week, I only went to the top deck three times a day for roll call, then I would climb back into my truck and think about home.

Slowly I began to mentally metamorphosis from the sound of the shotgun blast torturing my murky subconscious, the sound became more dense with each passing day. I made my way up the metal steps clinging to the hand railing preventing myself from slamming into the bulkhead because of the violent rocking of the ship. Peeking over the top rail of the steps, the sun greeded me with a blinding light, suggestly saying, "Weak up, your alive." I made my way onto the deck, and for the first time in two weeks, I could see birds landing on the bowel of the ship. I knew we were within eyesight of land and right before I could complete the thought a city emerged out of nowhere.

I can recognize the sky line of San Diego from 100 miles away, it was the most beautiful site I've ever seen. I was grateful to see the coast once again. Every minute it took to approach the shore it seemed like an hour as the ship slowly dock. We unloaded our trucks and other equipment then convoy back to camp Pendleton. The long trip home was physically draining, we were too tired to hang signs out of the back of the trucks asking women to show their breast, before we making it back to the base rumors that one Marine walked in and caught his wife having sex with three men at the same time. Infidelity was very common around base housing units, husbands away for months at a time, while young navie wife's sit idely at home waiting for their return. It was the closest thing to Peyton Place I've ever seen.

At last we were back in the familiar and secured surroundings of our base,after rushing to secured our gear we were awarded a 72, meaning we had three days of liberty. I spent my 72 hours relaxing, stretching my feet across the front room table and for the moment I forgot about Beirut. I placed my short live combat tragedies deep in my subconscious and wouldn't speak of them again for 40 years.

Even though Cindy was not home I couldn't wait to get in the house and allow euphoria to set in. The house was quiet almost to the point of being ghostly, there was no laughter of children, not so much as a mouse squeak, but my neighbors were loud and up notches, letting their children run wild on the playground unsupervised, seemingly only hearing and not seeing them. I sat quietly on the porch sipping on a beer, free from the thought of Amtrak's and tanks rolling pass my head or an aircraft spraying me with CS gas, or the dead soldier staring up at the sky on the dark desolate winding road in Lebanon. I was in a moment of euphoria and all the sudden out walked an attractive young Puerto Rican girl seemingly focused on herself, cleaning and grooming her fingers and toe nails to perfection, looking as if they were professionally manicured. Her small 5 foot frame was athletic and well proportion. The red tube top she wore could barely contain her 36 double 'D' breast. I looked at her like a man in the desert staring at the last osais of fresh spring water for the first time.

I knew if I stared long enough she would become my next mistake, so I reluctantly got up and went in the house, shut the door, grab another beer, and plopped down on the couch for another episode of the Andy Griffin show. My friend Richie came by later that evening to borrow my car and ask if I wanted to go to the night club with him. I said, "No" "I just want to stay home and relax and listen to the sound of crickets playing below my window and allow the cool breeze of the california wind blow therapeuticly over my sand damaged face.

The breeze felt so good blowing through the window I walked outside and stook my place on front porch, once again, the breeze on my face was suddenly blocked. I looked up and their she was, standing 2 feet from me with a deck of poker cards in her hands.

She asked," do you want to play cards", "we can play goldfish" I said, " No, I just want to sit here quietly".

She was persistent. She asked three times in an insidious way, this time bending over hanging her huge 36 double D's in my face, my eyes went cross as her breast hung less than an inch from my mouth. It was all I could take so I reluctantly caved like a stack of dominoes, drunkly by her well proportioned body, I submitted to playing cards with her. There was nothing I could do at that point in time, the blood had already left my head, so I was no longer thinking clearly. I couldn't get up and run in the house because the blood left my feet as well and began to centralize once again in my pelvic region. I was in a temporary trans, I didn't know if it was her playing skill or my lack of focus on the game, but she beat me five games straight, I found it hard to concentrate on anything but her perfect body. She was killing me, I couldn't take it any more so I excused myself and limped into the house, closed the door leaving her on the porch to play solitaire by herself.

I must admit that I am weak for the flesh and I loved wild passionate uncontrollable sex but I was certainly no lothario. Five minutes later there was a knock at the door, she was definitely indomitable, their she stood with a bowl of blueberry pie.

"Would you like some pie" she asked. "No, I'm good, I'm just going to watch TV.

'Are you sure? It's really good" she said.

Asking over and over and over again. I began to have visions of smearing blueberry pie all of her huge naked breasts, so I submitted to her request once again. I open the door and walked out on the porch. We ate blueberry pie with a scoop of vanilla ice cream, my imagination run even wilder, we talked for about an hour.

Once again I excused myself and limped my way inside the house, this time I close the door to ensure that no one would bother me. Once again she was knocking on my door, I pull the curtain back and peeked out the window, this time she had nothing to offer, so I let her knock on my door two more times, before she could knock the third time I'd open the door grabbed her by her tube top and pulled her into the house.

The sexual experience mint nothing to me it was just another proverbial $15 on the table and no emotions required.

I never heard from her again, but Unbeknownst to myself her sister-in-law was listening at the door, she could hear the yelling and moaning as I was breaking her young sister in law off something proper. The next week after pulverizing my opponent in a boxing match I was walking down the side walk toward my house when the young girl older brother was coming down the side walk from the opposite direction with his wife. His wife was clutching his arm, digging her finger nails into his flesh preventing him from attacking me.

I wasn't worried because I knew he saw the first marine division championship boxing trophy in my hand and realize that he could get the brakes beat off his dumb ass, so he just walked by looking angrily at me out of the corner of his eye. Our sexual escapade would never happened again, soon after, her brother was discharged from the Marines within three months of our xxx one night stand.

Cindy return home shortly after, by this time she was more than seven months pregnant with our second child and more than ready to drop this load. I did feel guilty about my sexual promiscuous. I didn't have any real excuses for messing around, I suppose I just did it because I could. Most of the time I thought I cheated because I got married too young, or it was because I was like my father, or I was just bored, or it was because I wasn't in love when I got married. I was trying to do the honorable thing by marrying her, at the time I thought the honorable thing was the only way.

Our life became routine, going shopping on the weekends, walking on the beach or walking around the part of the base called main side located near the PX. We took pictures standing in front of the armored tanks and later that day we drove from one end of the base to the other just taking in the sights. One morning I was getting dress for work.

Cindy casually said, "My water broke, I am having the baby", She said it so calmly I didn't believe her so I kept getting dress.

She said, said "'take care of Michaela I'm going to the MP gate for an ambulance. I got dressed and hurried Michaela to the baby sitters, by the time I got to the MP gate she was gone. Miya was born November 25, 1980, in the Naval hospital on the Marine Corp base Camp Pendleton.

She had dark black eyes with Beautiful curly hair, most people thought she was a Hispanic baby, She was the first in my family to be born in another state are on a military base. Cindy and I were very happy and content with our life style, we attend church every Sunday one block from our base housing unit. Miya was the star of our church. Everyone wanted to hold her, before I new it she was on the other side of the church, being passed around from women to women, I traveled to teh otherside of the church to go retrieve her from some women I had never seen before. I must say she was an attractive little girl with curly coal black hair, and big black eyes.

I believe those were just old family genetics popping up to say we're still around. I didn't think I could make something so beautiful all by myself. After all the excitement of church I forgot It was Easter Sunday and I was supposed to be sitting at the barracks behind a desk as the duty NCO. I totally rebelled against the idea of standing duty after 12 weeks of being in the desert and spending a month aboard ship as well as being in another country. I knew I would have to pay the consequences for not showing up too stand my Post but I also knew the Gunnery Sgt. was wrong for continuously placing me on duty every weekend. After returning home from church I was informed by one of my friends that the first sergeant was banging on my door, I knew at that moment they were going to try and court-martial me when I arrive at work the next morning.

I arrived at the base anticipating the worst, before I could get in formation the first sergeant called me into his office.

"Stand at attention!" he yelled.

Reaching into his desk he pulled out a short three foot wooden club then slammed it on his desk. He stared at me as if he want to kill me, while rolling up his sleeves.

"I'm going to kick your ass!" he said. "Where the hell were you Sunday?" I stared at him for brief a second.

"I'm not afraid of you first sergeant". i said. He yelled. "Stand at ease".

Then he marched out of the room into the Captains office next door.

"Report to your Capt". He yelled.

I came to attention and marched into the captains office. "Go back out and report in right!", the first Sgt. said.

I did an about face, walked outside, then pounded heavily on the hatch.

"Sir, Cpl. Gray reporting as requested sir!

Captain, "Why didn't you report for duty on Sunday Cpl. Gray?'

"The gunnery Sgt. Repeatedly put me on duty every Sunday for the last two months and all the other NCOs have duty one weekend per month" I said.

Captain "well that's no excuse".

I said, "Sir before we go any farther I would like to request mass to see the commanding general".

Captain, "Step outside Cpl. Gray."

I stood outside for two minutes that same like an hour after which time I was order back into the office. They decided to give me duty one more Sunday before I was discharged. I began packing my house and return the furniture to base housing and the rental stores. I sold my car for slightly more than I paid for it, therefore, I spent the next six months riding my bike to and from work, 14 miles each way. The road was long, hilly and dark, my power generator light provided very little reflection making the ride more difficult while the wheel of generator rub against the back tire creating energy for the light. I tried to cover the hard Bicycle seat with a specially designed seat cover made of rabbit skin, but to no avail, my testicles banged against the seat likeball in a pinball machine. By the time I got to work it was time for morning PT.

Physical fitness training, included 80 sit up's, 20 pull-up's, jumping jacks and a 3 to 6 mile run. I ran my last (PFT), physical fitness test without motivation as if I didn't care, my platoon leader yelled at me as I just about walked across the finish line, completing the 3 mile run in 22 minutes.

"You're not even sweating" he yelled.

I just looked at him and walked over to the barracks. I was a short timer with less than three months left in the corp and I knew there was nothing he could do to help or hurt me. Three months later I had served my four years and my contract was over. I reported to the main Side base at camp Pendleton to receive my Final pay and discharge papers. Their must've been over 50 of us getting discharged that day, we were so happy, we stagger the line and talk loudly about our civilian plans. A Sgt. began started yelling from the top of the steps.

"Shut the fuck up and get in a straight line!".

The voice was so distinctive I recognize it right off. It was Sgt. Hondo, he had returned to his old job in finance, no longer was a drill instructor. After waiting 45 minutes I stepped in front of his window and said,

"Sgt. Hondo".

He looked up at me with a stern look and said, "Were you one of mine's"?

"Yes, sir platoon 1059".

I couldn't help but feel good seeing the beginning and the end come together. I smiled as I went down the steps after receiving my final pay and completing my final act in the Marine Corps. Just seeing my drill instructor again reminded me of what I had achieved.

I was discharged from the United States Marine Corps with an honorable discharge and returned to civilian life ready to be placed in a job I thought, I rightfully earned, but I soon found out that was not the case. I spent the first couple of weeks back in civilian life walking around the old neighborhoods on Delaware st. and Park ave, reminiscing about old times. I walked past John's old house on Washington Boulevard, remembering it wasn't long ago that I sat on his steps begging for candy.

I even took an occasional trip to riverside park hoping to catch a glimpse old friends. I didn't have a car, so I just rode the bus every where I traveled, enjoying the nice quiet ride while touring through familiar places. I even passed Saul Subway, I couldn't help but to stop and peek in the window. It Had only been four years that I was away but it seems like so much had changed, the only thing that remained the same was my family. They worked the same jobs, living the same life style, not traveling, or making any big plans, they just continue to live the same day in and day out routine. All of a sudden it appeared to me, I could see why I left Indianapolis.

The routine was stale and the City seemed slow and less progressive than California. Jobs were very scarce and I was in for a big surprise when I went looking for one. I thought being in the Marine Corps would give me the advantage, employers would just love to have a young fresh marine straight out of the military. I couldn't have been more wrong, no one cared that I was an ex-marine. I was just like everyone else, if you didn't have a skill or a college degree you didn't have a job.

I worked in field artillery for four years and had trouble matching my skills with any civilian employers qualifications, therefore; Civilian life was a big adjustment. I had to get use to unorganized and slow moving civilian behavior, the other bad news was we didn't prepare for the move back home so we moved in with Cindy's mother until we could find our own place.

I wasn't overjoyed with the decision so I hung out at my mother's house most of the time. Miya was too young so she stayed at home with her mother while Michaela went with me to the park and to play in her grand mothers backyard with her cousins. I hung out in the front yard with my brothers drinking beer and talking about old times. Cindy called two hours later requesting that I bring Michaela home to eat dinner. I didn't think much of it so back over the bridge I went to her mother's house. I found it difficult to stay in a strange place not knowing whether I was really welcome, but it seemed Cindy was right at home, cooking dinner and seemingly more alive then she was just a week ago in her own home. Her conversations had more of a edge to them, because her mother play with her mind. She tormented Cindy with conversations about my escapades in Japan and how I probably left children in Japan waiting to come to United States.

I didn't think it was funny at all, as a matter of fact I believe Cindy was taking her mother serious and began to show signs of jealous impulse. Any time I left home she wanted to go with me, even a casual stroll a half block down the street to the variety store she want to go with me. I was beginning to feel smothered and overwhelmed by the entire situation, so I escaped into myself playing with my kids on the couch and riding them on my back around the room. I looked through the newspaper everyday for work but was sadly disappointed by the lack of job opportunities in the capital city. I began to pound the pavement, newspaper tucked under my arm. I wanted to impress employers so I wore a pair of Stacy Adams and a pin strip suit I had made while station in Japan.

I headed to the downtown circle where multiple businesses lined the Streets. I when door-to- door but had little luck finding a job, but the day wasn't a total waste. I bump into a couple of old flames from my high school days, they saw my wedding ring on my finger, but didn't seem to care if I was married and invited me to come by after hours.

They even gave me their phone numbers but I drop them in the trash before I reached home. I didn't need any more drama in my life than I already had. I escaped unscathed from my extra marital affair with the Puerto Rican girl and I just didn't need the hassle, so I kept pressing forward trying to find a job. After several days of walking around I just couldn't get any traction, I wasn't making any ground because most of the jobs have moved to Carmel Indiana or out toward 86 street. I was destitute, without a car, securing a job was next to impossible.

I returned home that evening less confident than I was before I left. Fortunately for me my wife was big on saving money but we had to dip into our savings account sooner are later. We discuss buying the car Cindy's Brother had for sale, a 1976 Burgundy Cutlass Supreme with a half white top and burgundy crushed velvet interior. Her brother kept the car in immaculate condition, the paint was flawless as well as the inside of the vehicle. He wanted two thousand dollars but I waved $1600 in his face, he didn't even break stride as he ran across the room grabbing the cash, tossing me the keys as he walked into a corner to count his new found wealth. I couldn't wait to take the car for a spin and to my surprise Cindy let me take off by myself. I drove to my mothers house showing off the car to my brothers. My eldest brother Rayford con me into buying two old antiquated speakers, he even made an honest attempt to install the speakers but hardly had a clue how to mount them properly in the back of the car. It took three hours and finally they were installed. My sister Sherry yelled out the door, Cindy wants you on the phone, she said bring the car back to the house.

I thought to myself, "now, it starts" I didn't want to look like I was weak are hen pecked by my wife so I hung out for another hour with my brothers, besides I haven't seen them in 18 months. After downing a couple more beers I headed back to Cindy's mothers house. I was greeted at the door with low key aggression as I stepped onto the back porch. Cindy reaching and clawing trying to snatch the keys out of my hand, I shoved the keys deep inside my pocket follow by her hand probing deep into the pelvic region of my pants trying to retrieve the keys. She won that battle, she ran upstairs and hid the keys in a secure place insuring that I would not journey out of the house again that night.

I could understand how she felt but little did she know the more she tried to control me the more she pushed me away, after spending four years in the Marines I wasn't taking any more orders from anyone else. I didn't like being controlled nor did I understand why her mother felt it necessary to talk about me going back to Japan to be with Asian women, it didn't make sense. I thought she was childish and insensitive and only serve the purpose to make Cindy angry. Cindy became more and more of a Klingon, refusing to detach herself from my every move. I felt the walls closing in on me. I laid in the bed staring at the ceiling while everyone else slept peacefully. Sleep deprivation sat in, as my eyes were gluded to the celing. I laid in bed listening to the mouse traps snapping the necks of mice foraging for food. I felt totally out of place so I walked downstairs in the middle of the night, staring out the front window onto the quiet peaceful but unsafe streets of 25th and central avenue.

I knew somewhere among all those thousands of buildings, there had to be a job for me. I felt responsible for my children, I wanted them to live in their own house, sleep in their on bedrooms and eat what they want without having to ask permission from their grandmother. I want my wife to be the woman of her own home and not feel as though she has to tolerate the behavior of her crazy ass mother. Occasionally Cindy showed little respect for her mother, engaging in toe to toe arguments, something my mother would never let me get away with, and I would never disrespect my mother in that manner in the first place. For the most part I thought Cindy was a sweet loving girl until someone did something to rattle her cage.

I began to grow increasingly tired of staying around the house day in and day out. I didn't have a life and it was getting old quick, fast and in a hurry, but Cindy love the ideal of me being around the house day after day, 24 hours a day. She loved having me within eye distance and all to herself. I went along with it for as long as I could but like' popeye' I couldn't stand it anymore, so I grabbed the car keys and off I went cruising around Parks, hanging out with buddies that I hadn't seen in years. I played a few games of basketball, drink a couple of beers. Just as I was beginning to feel good about my new found freedom it wasn't long before Cindy grew leary of my absence. In a fit of rage she walked over to the park, concealing herself well behind big oak trees and waited for the right moment. I turn my back to run to the other end of basketball court, then she made her move. She ran to the park bench grabbing my car keys, she jumped into the car and fled back across the bridge toward her mother's house.

I ignore her for the most part because I knew she wasn't going anywhere out of reach so I continued to play basketball until everyone decided to end the game for the night. I was somewhat embarrassed as everyone jumped in their cars and headed off while I had to reluctantly walk home to a place I didn't want to be. I stepped through the front door, the House was very quiet to the point of being eerie, normally her mother is repeatedly listening to renditions of the song 'clean up woman'. I didn't even smell her cigarette smoke or food cooking in the kitchen. The house was surprisingly quiet, I asked myself, "Where are the kids. I noticed the keys lying on the fireplace, before I couldn't reach them Cindy beat me to the punch, she ran around the chair and jumped over the back of the couch. Without breaking stride she very athletically snatched the keys off the mantle all in one motion. She stuffed the keys in her pocket, wink at me, give me a half smile then Pranced her way into the kitchen, summonings me with her finger to the dinner table.

The meal was exiguous, a pair of pigs feet laced with bar-bare cue sauce, macaroni and cheese and collard greens. I thought this meal should be served on Sunday considering it was the beginning of the week. I set at the table and watched Cindy's youngest sister devour her pig feet, bite after bite, ripping the skin away from the bone like A carnivorous prehistoric animal. Cindy prepared a plate of two pig feet and all the trimmings, then proudly slit the food in front of me as though she had prepared a meal fit for a King. I didn't want to be ungrateful but, hell will freeze over before I ate those big feet. A knock at the door temporarily distracted Cindy so she left the room for a split second giving me time to shove the pig feet back into the pan, her younger sister watched as I slid the pig feet off my plate settling deep into the barbecue sauce.

"Here,' I said, you can have another pigs feet go-ahead take it.

She grabbed the pig feet with her baby hands, and within seconds she began ripping meat right off the bone.

I gave her a half smile and pat her on head. I put my finger to my mouth signaling her not to tell. I didn't want to hurt Cindy feelings, she was from Mississippi and pigs feet was their traditional type of meal. I had never eaten pig feet in my life, as a matter of fact I have never seen a real pigs foot on anyone's plate before that night. I only saw pigs feet attached to the pigs bodies. The macaroni and cheese was filling enough for me, so I retired upstairs and Cindy followed close behind being ever so demonstrative, slapping me on my butt as I climb the stairs to our room. We sat on our bed occupied by nothing but time, we talked and try to come to a decision about the use of the car.

I felt it was my car because I used my money to purchase the car. Cindy was very pugnacious by nature she couldn't let go of an argument until she believed she won, and other times she would have an affable personality. I told her "I don't care about what she thought, I was going to do what I want" I slipped my pants off and laid back on the bed in my boxer shorts. Cindy casually got up and disappeared into the hallway. I didn't trust her, I knew to stay awake even if I have to use my night vision technique. Several minutes later she came back into the room wearing a provocative nightgown totally distracting me from any signs of danger, but I noticed she had one hand behind the her back. She slowly caress my thighs and before I know it she grabbed my penis as if her hands were a pair of vice grips with locking channels, she pressed a razor sharp meat cleaver against my penis.

I didn't care whether she was seriously or not her wish was my command, at that point she totally had me by the balls "literally". I couldn't move or barely breathe, she looked at me with vengeful eyes as she grind her teeth, she leaned forward and whispered in my ear.

"I ought to cut your Dick off".

I jokingly reply" then you won't get any either".

She press the meat cleaver deeper into my flesh angle down as though to make a final cut. She began to draw blood then I let out a hi Octavio Yell that could wake the dead, she released my penis and toss me a towel while shoving the meat cleaver under the mattress. I thought to myself.

" I have agape Love for her but I'm not trying to die for it".

I got to my feet and hurried downstairs applying pressure to the wound, trying to stop the bleeding, Cindy came downstairs, place her head on my chest, laughing to herself she said,

"I'm sorry, you'll be okay baby".

To be honest her crazy ass turned me on but she was crazy to the 13th degree and I knew if I didn't get away from her she would do more physical damage and damage that may not be repairable. I didn't know what to do, I was at a total loss. I didn't want to leave my kids, although I trusted Cindy to raise our girls in the past but now I was beginning to have serious doubts about her mental state of mind. She definitely appeared to be quick to anger but she could always sucker me back in two minutes after our fight, once she's back to being the sweet angel that I met outside of Saul's subway. She knew where to touch me, and how to touch me, and what to say when she was touching me, yes she had my number and she knew it. I stayed awake most nights thinking about our marriage and how long can I go on facing knives every time we had a minor disagreement.

I just didn't know what to do. I was very attached to Michaela but I haven't yet had a chance to bond with Miya. For some strange reason I knew our marriage wouldn't last because Cindy was still mentally wounded by my sexual escapades in Japan. I didn't know what to say or how to say it. Every time we made love she commented on how much better I was at having sex after I return from Japan, therefore; I must've been having sex with a lot of women to develop that kind of sexual prowess. I was pleased that she thought I was good in bed, but I was tired of sleeping with one eye open. I was no longer in the Marines, there was no reason to conserve my night vision by closing one eye while keeping the other one open. I slept with both hands covering my growing, I even thought about wearing a jock strap with a protective cup. Sleeping nude with this woman was a thing of the past, I went to bed fully clothed and slept on my stomach with one eye wide open, scanning the area for meat cleavers or flying knives.

Over the next several months I tried everything to be on my best behavior, I stayed at home, not only at home but in the house, only going on the front porch and occasionally to the variety store within eyeshot from the front porch. I wanted our marriage to work so I was willing to sacrifice myself but there was one small problem. I needed a job. I couldn't stand being caged in, depression slowly creeped into my murky subconscious. I felt as though I was losing myself for another human being. I felt trapped and couldn't breathe because the walls of un-marital blizz were closing in. It was the month of August and I had been out of the military 30 days, my travel had been limited to my mothers house and back home.

I couldn't take it anymore so I took off walking until I walked the boredom out of my system. I walked up to school #60 just to sit on the steps and reminisce about my childhood. I didn't know how long I was gone or how far I went I just kept walking. Finally I arrive back home three hours later. Cindy was standing in the kitchen with a scarf tied around her head. She stood at the stove boiling hot water with a box of grits in her hand.

She said" these or for you"

I said to myself". I never had grits before this might be a nice change"

I sat on the couch anticipating eating something other than pig feet for once. Five minutes later Cindy came around the corner with a pot of boiling grits and before I know it she was drawing back to throw the grits at me. I flipped over out-of-the-way just as the grits splash on the wall. I try to get to my feet but I slipped in the grits and fell back to the floor on one knee, before I could stand up she came charging out of the kitchen with a butcher knife. Something clicked in me as though it was an automatic reaction. I grabbed her knife wheeling hand and flipped her over my back disarming her of the butcher knife. I tossed the knife on the floor and made my escape out the back door while her brother held her long enough for me to get in my car and drive off. I truly don't think she would've hurt me with the knife but I wasn't going to stay around and find out.

I believe most of the time she was just acting out, putting on a show for her mother or whatever family members she can use as an audience, but unfortunately for her I grew very tired of being in survival mode all the time. I spent one night at my mothers house which didn't make any difference in regard to my sleep deprivation. I still stared out the door at 4 AM, my mind raced like the cars in the Indy 500. I couldn't hold a single thought in my head, I worry about everything, work, or where I will be 20 years from now, my marriage, and mostly about my children. I knew deep inside I couldn't stay away from Cindy no matter how crazy she was, I've grown to love her and it deeply saddened me that we were apart, it bother me more not knowing if we would ever repair our marriage.

I spent the next several months living in my oldest brother apartment, off 38th St. We were living the bachelors life, he had an occasional girlfriend spend the night and I had an occasional old flame from my boxing days drop in for a night of sexual ecstasy. I wasn't mentally attached to any of them, my mind was still on my wife, so I shared with all the women before any sex took place that I was married and wasn't going to leave her. I didn't care how they felt or if I hurt their feelings because it was just sex, a cliché, something for the moment and nothing more. I wanted to give my marriage another chance. Cindy would have to prove her anger was under control and she let go of my past sexual escapade in Japan as I let go of her pass sexual relationship she had with her old boyfriend when I was in Japan.

He live conveniently across the street from her mother lees than 30 feet away. She had sex with one person and I had sex with many and I believe that's what upsets her. After endless months of scouring the newspapers and pounding the pavement I was hired for the graveyard shift as a security guard at a helicopter engine manufacturing plant. It was definitely the good old boys club and I knew in certain terms, I wasn't welcome, they were just filling a quota by giving me the job, either way I didn't care. I just wanted to work. I never thought it would be this difficult for veterans to find a job. I was under the illusion that veterans had preference.

That fantasy flew out the window along with all the other idiocies that I learned about being a patriot, serving in the military and waving the American flag with pride. My military service didn't mean much to employers and it was beginning to mean even less to me. I spent four years operating million dollars worth of equipment, firing artillery shells over the head of troops, coordinating fire as section chief of a 12 man crew server weapon, but none of this could be applied to a civilian occupation. I received $1 million worth of training in the military, but the training was valued at $3.25 an hour in the civilian world. I walked around the helicopter plant as though I was standing guard duty on a military post, the meter clock neatly strapped to my shoulder, my clothes were finely pressed, my choler fram shoes were buffed to a high gloss.

Every hour I would cruise through the planet. When one guard return to the guard booth the other guards would walk around the planet, punching his clock at selective stations. I hated this job but I had to support myself and my children. I stopped by every weekend to visit with my kids, Cindy was on her best behavior because she wanted me to return home but I was still skeptical of her unmanaged and displaced anger. So I visit my kids then back to my brothers house for a night of running the streets and club hopping. Those nights were beginning to remind me of my old days in Japan, I was free to do what I want and I didn't have to answer to anybody as long as I came back to the base sober. All the club hopping we did didn't amount to much. I never picked up a Woman in any of the clubs and over a period of time I was beginning to lose interest. I start staying around the house more. I worked, I went home and every weekend I would visit my kids and take them to the park. I felt empty inside I want to be with my wife but I didn't want to get into a fisticuffs..

One day out of nowhere it started pouring down rain, the rain was so heavy I was forced to pull to the side of the road. After five minutes the rain begin to lighten, I still could only see 20 feet in front of me, so I drove slow and cautiously taking my time because I have nothing to do and nowhere to go. I saw someone standing on the bus stop in the pouring rain wearing white pants, totally drenched, soaking wet from head to toe. I pulled over and asked her if she would like a ride.

She said, "No thank you".

I said, "Stop playing and get in this car".

Suddenly lightning crack across the sky like a whip, she folded her umbrella then quickly jumped into the car. She removed her scarf. She was young and attractive I wanted to see where she lived, so I offer to give her a ride all the way home. In my mind I thought she live where every other struggling young adult lived, in the Grass Moore Apartments, but she lived on 38th and Emerson much further than I could afford to go so I looked at her, then at my gas gage. I had a fourth of a tank of gas and I didn't want to waste it on someone I had no intimate connection with, but I was overtaken by the size of her perfectly round butt and I wanted to see more so I sacrificed my last drop of gas so I could sneak a peek.

I slowly creep up to the front of her apartment taking my time to make the day last a little bit longer. We sat and talked until the rain stopped, she hopped out of the car and made her way down the long sidewalk toward her Apartment door. She waved goodbye but I didn't move an inch, I was too busy watching her wide 40 inch Butt switch back-and-forth. She looked back over her shoulders to see if I was enjoying the view. I was not only enjoying the view, I was in total amazement, once again the blood left my feet and my brain, centralizing in my pelvic region. I got dizzy but was able to refocus before driving off. I knew when and where to pick her up so I made it a habit to cruise by her job everyday in the same place at the same time. I was very friendly, lets make no mistake about it, I wasn't simply rescuing her from a bus stop, I was trying to take one for the team. We dated four weeks but she wasn't giving me any signals about the direction our relationship was going.

I begin to wonder if I was wasting my money and my time on her, she was eating me out of house and home. She eat McDonald's barbecue rib sandwiches by the pound, savoring every bite. I bought her three barbecue rib sandwiches on three different days and still she didn't even let me smell her panties. I was getting sick of her begging ass, she was getting free meals and free transportation home everyday, our relationship was purely platonic, built on barbecue sandwiches. The onus was on her to make the first move. To my surprise she invited me into her dim lit studio apartment she shared with her brother. The apartment was arranged like any young persons apartment, quite empty, nothing on the walls, a mildly worn out couch placed in the middle of the room and a love seat shoved in the corner was the only piece of furniture occupying the tiny apartment.

The peep hole on the door was jammed with a wod of paper to prevent anyone from looking inside. The apartment was dimly lit as if they were trying to save money on their electric bill. We sat close on the couch and talked for what seemed like hours. I was close enough to her I could smell the absence of perfume on her body, her lips were chap and dry and she squinted her eyes as she bit into the cold barbecue rib sandwich she had left from the day before. She offered me a bite but I shook my head no, she savor every bite, as if she hasn't had a meal in weeks. She let out a belch wiping the barbecue sauce from her mouth with her sleeve then headed into the bathroom closing the door behind her.

I sat anxiously on the couch anticipating her next move. The bathroom door was slightly ajar I could see her reflection in the mirror, first she took off her blouse, then her pants, my eye bulged out of my head intensify each moment as I watched her like a peeping Tom. She undress all the way down to her black satin panties, clinging to her beautiful brown skin. I move to the edge of couch pertending as if I had no interest. I wanted so bad to shove the bathroom door open and claim my prize, but I was going to be a gentleman that night, so I waited patiently for her to invite into the den of iniquity.

Suddenly I was summonsed to the bathroom, I leaped through the bathroom door as though I was shot out of a cannon, pushing the door back she was lying in the tub naked as a Jaybird, body shaped like an hour glass, with smooth skin like Queen Nefertiti. She reached up grabbed my hand.

"Take off your clothes and get in." She said, but I was too shy to comply with what she was asking. The apartment is too small, I had no where to escape too if her brother walked in.

"No I don't feel comfortable and what if your brother comes home" I said. She pulled me closer.

"Don't worry about him he always comes in late".

I still didn't get in the tub but I did help her dry off, taking my sweet time, rubbing the towel all over every inch of her well proportioned body, my sexual appetite was being fed large doses of sinful flesh.

I felt her warm breath on my neck, I became so concupiscence my eyes went cross and I loss conscious for a couple of seconds. When I came too, their she was standing in front of me disrobed, her beautiful brown skin on display, not a blemish are unsightly mark to be found, her coal black hair hung slightly past her shoulder only serve to accentuate her hour glass Frame. My weekly investment no longer felt the financial loss of three barbecue ribs sandwiches, I was about to get paid in full and with dividends. It was my birthday I believe that was the reason she let me make love to her or a better term, break her off something proper.

I didn't love her at least not yet, we were getting acquainted with one another, one sexual episode at a time. I didn't know if I would ever love her, I was still married and had no intention of leaving my children for her or any other women, as bad as my marriage was I still thought about Cindy and my two girls all the time. I wasn't a perfect husband but I wanted to be a perfect dad. After several months of dating, Gina and I moved in together. I don't know what the hell I was thinking or if I was thinking at all. She was so toothsome and voluptuous my hormones ran wild, not allowing me to think clearly, not with common sense anyway.

My little head did all the thinking, while my big head floated in time and space like an abandoned space station.

Gina and I were both very fortunate to have full-time jobs, our combining incomes didn't even equal $10 dollars an hour. I work for a security company and she worked at a dental office making false teeth. We were just getting by for a while, we went to the movies regularly, and out to dinner on several occasions. I got to meet a few of her girlfriends. One girlfriend in particular (Pat) Gina thought I was having an affair with her but there was nothing between us. She was attractive, very well groomed as if she lived a beauty shop. She had a long slender body with big 36 double D breast. I could see why Gina was a little jealous, it was competition and Gina knew what parts of women l liked. Pat would often come over strutting around the apartment wearing tight blue jeans and her stylus white silk shirt, showing off her figure, knowingly driving me crazy while she set on the end of the couch allowing the sunlight to penetrate through her shirt, giving me a view of what she thought I was missing. After six months of living together I lost my job and so did Gina, and to make the situation worse my car transmission stop working right in front of a transmission shop. I had no choice but to push the Car onto the lot. The Shop wanted $400 to repair the car, which didn't seem like a lot of money but I didn't have two nickels to rub together so I left the car at the transmission repair shop and walked 6 miles home.

Gina and I spent the summer searching for jobs. Neither of us had any formal training or education, therefore; I was restricted to work for manpower day labor, she work various jobs throughout the city never finding steady work. We got bored sitting around the house so our sex life blossom, we fornicated practically everyday, sometimes twice a day. Our refrigerator was empty but somehow we seemed to be able to feed ourselves at least once a day. I found myself walking everyday looking for work, sometimes I walked 7 to 8 miles each day wearing a three piece suit and Stacy Adams shoes.

Once I took a bus to apply for a bus boy job at a popular restaurant on the East side of town, to my surprise their was a line of people stretched around the corner for one busboy position, the word got out that someone already got hired for the position through nepotism. I couldn't believe it, I'd come all this way for nothing, no money in my pocket, 85° outside and I have to walk home from 56th and Keystone to 30th and Post Road. I was tired of being broke, not having a penny in my pocket. I needed my car out of the shop so I could expand my job search.

Frustration and despair was written all over my face, I sat outside on my apartment steps contemplating about my life and where I would get the money from to get my car out of the shop. I went for a walk around the block to clear my head. I couldn't help but notice that one man was working at the gas station by himself and then it hit me, that's how I can get some money. Rob this gas station, but as I recalled, my father tried robbing a bank with little success. I thought for the monment I was out of options. I had not yet vision my future, I could only see what was in front of me. The pain of being poor, uneducated and with out hope. I didn't understand who I was and what great future awaited me.

The next day I walk to my brother Denton's apartment. We sat and talked for a while before he offered me one of his generic beers.

I said, "Sure I'll have one".

I opened the refrigerator door and to my surprise all the refrig was well organized, all the cans were yellow with one big word on the can written in large back letters.

"My lord" I said. "I tasted nothing but barley".

I held the can of beer up in the air and stared at it, there were no inscriptions on the can other than the word "beer". I try to drink it, making polite conversation then ask if I could borrow his gun. He didn't ask any questions, he open the gun chamber to ensure it was loaded, closed the chamber and handed me the gun.

All that day I cased the gas station across street from the apartment complex that set parallel to teh gas station. I watch the movement of the men inside, one man went home and the other stayed to close the stop. "This is it" I thought to myself putting my ski mask on my head. I slowly made my way across the street towards the gas station. I opened the Chamber of a gun to ensure that it was ready, suddenly the chamberfail to the ground and the bullets scattered all over the sidewalk.

It took me several minutes to recover the bullets, by that time I could see clearly this was the wrong thing to do, so I put the gun away and walked back to my brothers house. I set on the balcony and drink

89

one of his generic beers and handed him back his gun. My ancestors were working over time, it was divine intervention, I was given a second chance to become the person I was created to be. Within seconds my life came to a halt, the divine forces at the sub- atomic level radiated form the crust of the earth turning me 180 degrees in the opposite direction. i didn't know where I was going or how I was going to get there but I was on my way to my manifest destination with God at the wheel. I've only ran away from one challenge, 'education' but it was time for me to face the elephant in the room. My life wasn't going to change unless I stepped into the reality of my future, seeing where I wanted to go and be in the next 10 years. A question mark linger over my head like a cloud with a spot of sun light, I didn't understand the drastic changes unknowingly coming my way. Changes that would remove me from my present living circumstances and thrust far from away from the path of least resistance. My soul screamed "let the journey begin," but my woke conscious said,

"I am fine I will stay where I am". The feeling of forward movement was overwhelming, things were starting to get uneasy around the apartment, our relationship had run its course. Gina and I was spending too much time together coupe up in our small apartment, we were beginning to slowly drift apart. Sex couldn't make up for the discontent in our relationship. I try to make our evenings more interesting by finding new ways to prepare eggs, the last bit of food we had in the house. Occasionally my eldest daughter spend the night. Cindy didn't want Michaela spending the night with me, but she let her come over anyway, but not without reciprocity. She wanted a full report once Michaela got home the next morning. but Michaela was to young dictate what she had witness. 6 AM the phone rang obnoxiously off the hook, it copuld only be one person, her anger seep through the phone like acid, my ears burned from the toxic yelling and venomous words, was Cindy requesting in a that I bring Michaela home right now. I told her I'll bring her home in two hours when I get up but she kept calling and calling until I agreed to take her home.

I arrived at Cindy's mothers house at around 7 AM I knocked on the door as thought I was reporting to my first sgt, turning the knob slowly the door open and I stepped inside the house,

"Go up and get in the bed Michaela". I said,

She ran towards the staircase reaching the top of the steps then stop and came back down midway, she set down on the steps and stared at me as if she was looking right through me. I waved bye to her and said.

"It"s okay baby go on up to bed".

She got up and made her way up the steps. At that moment Cindy step from behind the door, jumped on my back and place a butcher knife to my throat.

"I ought to cut your fucking head off".

She said, while applying pressure to the knife placed against my throat. In a split second I did what was natural for me to do, my mind clicked over and I flash back to my hand-to-hand combat training. I grabbed her knife wheeling hand, took one step back flipping Cindy over my shoulder onto the floor. I tossed the knife on the floor making a hasty exit for the door.

Before I could reach my car Cindy began throwing knives and bricks at me from the front porch. I stood there in awe, subconsciously blocking bricks harolding through the air, knifes, and even can good from rhe cabinet with my hands. She was out of control and I didn't know what else to do, so I walked up to her in uncontrol anger intending on slapping some sense into her but as I swung, my anger fused my hand shut, failing to open, I struck her just below her left eye with my fist.

I felt horrible, I felt so bad I grabbed her, hugging her and said. "I'm sorry I didn't mean to do that, I'll let you hit me back."

Before the words cleared my mouth she cold cocked me riht inhe eye, cutting my eye in almost the exact same place as hers, but she didn't stop there, she ran to the kitchen grabbing more knives from the kitchen drawer, giving me seconds to make my getaway, as I drove off she ran behind the car throwing bricks, barley missing my driver's door window as I skid around the corner. It would be a month before I made the conscious decision to visit my children again, the meeting would have to be in a mutual place, not at her mothers house.

I spent most of the summer looking for work struggling through the financial ruins of my life or spending unproductive idol time at my apartment. I was extremely bored, some days I would walk from post road to 29th and Talbott St. to visit my mother, then I would walk home later that day. The Marines prepared me for any physical obstacle I would meet in the civilian world, but not so much in the area of employment. My exit from the Marines didn't provide me with any transferable skills, everything I learned in the Marines or thought I knew I can't use in the civilian world. I was forced to look for low income jobs or to go to college, something I wasn't prepared to do.

I was struggling in all areas of my life, sprituality, mentally, financially, and relationship. The proverbial walls of civilian life were closing in on me. I couldn't see clearly which path to take or or how to began down any path of purpose, my compass for life direction was broken, my vision was blocked by my lack of believe in my abilities togrow in any area of my life. possibility. I was stuck. Here I was, I had just served my country for four years and I couldn't even get a job as a bus boy. The time we spent clamored in our small one bedroom apartment began to create an unrestful situation. Tensions grew as Gina and I began to really get on one another's nerves, the sex had run its course, she was young and inexperienced and couldn't take me sexually where I need to go. After having sex five or six times a day, in 3 to 4 hour sessions for six months straight, we both were bored with it. I begin to see another side of her, a very childish side of her personality that would irritate me to no end. She would do little things to try to pick a fight but I would just ignore her and watch TV.

One day she was picking with me just out of spite.

" I never see you get upset". "Get mad." I want to see you Get mad".

Little did she know I had a quite anger brewing inside of me,with an untrained release valve. I don't remember getting up, before I knew it I grabbed one of my Japanese swords off the stand on resting top of the TV, I stood outside my self and watch my alter-eagle move gracefully and deadly, I wasn't conconscious of my action, it was the long hours of stairing into the night in the across the ice cover rice patties in sub below weather of South Korea, waiting for the north to cross the border. My training taught me to be ready with an unconious thought, reserved for unwarranted or unexpected satuations. I put my Saber sword to her throat, her feet dangling freely in the air, I didn't notice I had her at knife point until I felt her tears streaming down my arm. I released her from my grasp, before her feet hit the floor she exploded in panic, immediately scrambling around the apartment throwing loose clothing in her suitcase.

She was moving so fast you would've thought she was in Boot Camp. Her friend Pat slid to a stop in front of the apartment, she stayed in her car looking up at me standing in the window clutching a sword, leaning against the frame of the dinning room window comsumed by the thousand yard stair. Afraid to come inside, frantically blowing her horn signaling Gina to bring her bags to the car. I continued to watch TV, hardly noticing she left until later that evening when loneliness consumed the empty spaces of the apartment. For the first time I was by myself and had time to think about what I was doing with this women and where was this relationship going. I decided to call it quits, I packed my bags and went home to my wife and kids.

My past experiences from the people around me taught me that repairing my marriage would not be easy, and it will get worse before it got better, but I had to try. I didn't want my children to grow up without my influence. I know what it feels like to be without a father and I made a promise to myself I would not abandon my children like my father did to myself and my siblings. He walked away from us abdicating his responsibility as a father. The child support bureaus where not as established in the 60s and 70s as they are today. The government didn't actively seek out and put fathers in jail for not providing support for their children, therefore; my mother was left to her own devices to figure it out. I harvest hate and grew a distaste in my mouth for my father and swore I would never abandon my children. I could be a better man but the question remains, was I mature enough to demonstrate the qualities I knew I possessed.

Cindy scour the newspapers until she founded the perfect two bedroom apartment on the westside of town, ten miles west of where we both worked full-time. Cindy found a job as a House keeper in the Indiana teachers Association building. I on the other hand became a "Special deputy sheriff", a fancy term for security guard with arrest powers. We were doing okay, we took our savings and purchase enough funiture to for the entire house. We settle nicely into our new apartment, turning into the nuclear family Cindy always dreamed about. Everything was going great until three months later the phone call that was heard around the world rang my phone. A call from Gina was all it took to turn my world upside down and inside out. She was pregnant.

"I want to money for an abortion"! She yelled.

I scramble around grathering cash like a pack of wolves in search of the last bit of food. Somehow I gather the money, took it to her apartment but she packed up lock stock and barrel, there wasn't a crumb to be found in the apartment, not even a crum from the cold cut sandwiches loved so much. I didn't know where she was so I made contact with a few of her close girlfriends, after three days of searching, one of her girlfriends finally confess that she moved to South Bend Indiana. I was infuriated, I drove down the street 60 miles an hour searching for the first phone booth in sight.

I spotted a phone booth tucked away in the corner on the Zaryes parking lot, the phone booth smelled of urine, the receiver was cracked, lingering with the smell of whiskey breath. But I didn't care I grabbed the phone frantically dialing her mother's number. After hidding three weeks, to my surprise, She answered.

"What do you want"? She asked,

"You know what I want, why didn't you tell me you were pregnant?" I said, "I did know at the time" she said.

"Are you coming back to Indianapolis?" I ask. "I thought you were going to get an abortion?" She angrily replied.

"No, I'm keeping it because I'm tired of you leaving me".

Then she slammed the recceiver down on the hook. I set in my car for an hour, thinking of what a mess I made of my life, what was Cindy going to think if she found out. I just couldn't take any more of her bipolar episodes but in this instance she'll be justified in whatever reaction she choose. I headed to my mother-in-law's house to pick up my children, then to Cindy's job to pick her up before we headed back to our apartment. That became our routine for the next 45 days. All of a sudden Cindy stop talking, I had not yet reveal to her Gina was pregnant, even though Cindy and I were separated for one year during that time of the pregnancy. I knew in Cindy's mind that wouldn't matter. It wouldn't matter if I left the planet and got an alien pregnant on the moon, it wouldn't change the situation or how she felt about the situation or how she would react to the situation.

Over the course of the next three days, our marriage took a turn for the worse. The atmosphere was ripe with anger, with every breath she took the situation intensify. Cindy started communicating physically rather than orally. One day I work the Graveyard shift at a trucking yard. After working eight hours I decided to stop downtown at the donut shop and treat myself to a cup of coffee and a donut, it was only five in the morning, very few people were up moving around on the snow covered streets. I sat quietly in the coffee shop with my back against the wall, seemingly enjoying my favorite past-time, (watching the world come alive, people arriving at work. Steam coming from the sewer, the pavement wet from the heavy foot traffic traffic.)Then I realized I have been sitting there for 30 minutes, so I gather my things and drove home. I walked in the door, I knew it!, she was totally predictable. My luggage and clothing bag laid on the front room floor. My luggage was sliced into little pieces, my clothes were sprawled all over the floor, as if they were kicked around. 10 seconds later, Cindy comes out of the bedroom steaming mad, yelling.

"Where the hell you been all morning."

I was too tired to respond, I just slumped on the couch and looked at her in disbelief. She said, "Get your stuff and get out."

I was to tired to argue are fight so I grab my bags, collected my clothes and headed for the door.

Cindy wasn't having it, she jumped in front of the door holding two butcher knives, one in each hand.

She said, "You can go, but you can't take the car." I looked at her with a puzzled look on my face.

"There's snow and ice everywhere, I know you don't expect me to walk out of here carrying this stuff in my hand, walking over ice and snow?" I said.

To my advantage the window was ground level, so I snatched open the window, throwing my bags and luggage into the back of the apartment. Getting through the window was a small obstacle to get around because I was still in peak condition from my military service. I picked my bags up and try to run to the car, by the time I got there, she had sliced three of my tires. She looked at me and said,

"Now you can go."

I knew there were gas stations nearby within two blocks, so I jumped in the car, threw the car in reverse trying to make it to the gas station before all the air went out of the tires. Before I knew it Cindy jumped on the hood of the car like a character from the zombie movie and started stabbing the windshield with a butcher knife. I kept driving as if she wasn't even there. I exit the apartment complex hitting ice, sliding sideways onto 38th Street, I turned left heading towards Lafayette Sq, Mall. I proceeded toward the gas stations two blocks away but I wasn't sure If I was going make it so I increased my speed to about 40 miles an hour. Cindy rode on the hood, clutching each windshield wiper helping her to maintain her balance as I did a U-turn into the parking lot of a tire repair station. Just as I came to a stop, three of the tires went flat. Cindy stood outside the car yelling, screaming and stabbing wildly at the drivers door window. I set in the car with my hand placed over the trigger of my 357 magnum. It was 6 o'clock in the morning and I thought to myself.

"it's too early for this shit".

Cindy stood unmovable in her Cotton nightgown with no shoes and a scarf wrapped around her head, clutching a 12 inch knife, yelling and screaming. She was so angry I don't even think she knew how cold it was.

She must've stood there for at lease an hour making threats, yelling at me to get out of the car. Suddenly Michaela began walking down the street. I could see her from a distance, I pointed in her direction. Cindy stopped her rage for the moment to take Michaela back in the house. I sat in the car in disbelief not even noticing seven hours have passed. At 3 PM Cindy came back to the car no longer angry. She offered me money for my tires.

She said, "I will not hurt you, it's okay if you sleep on the couch. She went back to the apartment and I set in the car for 30 more minutes wondering whether or not I should trust her. I went into the trunk of my car and took out my gun shoulder holster. I shove my magnum into the holster and put it under my jacket, leaving my bags in the car. I reluctantly headed back to the apartment for a sleepless night.

I was willing to do anything to be with my children but she was making it impossible for me to stay. I knew at this point she was bipolar and needed help but she had a real sweetness about her. It was hard for me to walk away from my marriage, so I stayed the night. I slept on the couch eyes wide shut, meaning, my eyes were closed but I was very conscious of any movement around the apartment. I felt like a stranger in my own home, not really welcome but just there to support other people and their agendas. The next morning Cindy walked into the room and toss rolled up bills onto the couch.

"This is for your tires." She said,

Laughing to herself struting down the hallway like a proud peacock. I unrolled the money, feeling a little sign of relief I was able to breath eaiser. It was only $25, I went from being at ease to full set on panic. I had to be at work in 7 hours.

I said, "What is this? How can I buy three tires with $25?"

She looked at me walking back-and-forth between the bedroom and kitchen, smiling and laughing to herself. She really didn't believe I would be able to repair the tires with only $25 and drive the car off, in her mind she had me beat, but I had other plans. While setting in the car earlier that day I noticed a stack of tires in a bend on the side of the building. I returned to my car and begin selectively pulling one tire at a time from the massive stack of hundreds of tires.

The tires seemed to be in pretty good shape, I couldn't understand why someone would discard perfectly good tires, these tires had good rubber and deep threads. As I pulled the tires out from the stack it seemed that one tire was better than the next. It was a gold mine of tires, I stacked three tires beside my car then jacket the car up and remove one tire at a time. Carrying the new tire and row the flat tire down the street four blocks in the snow and slush to the shell gas station. I was charged five dollars per tire to mount the tires on the rim. It was perfect, I couldn't believe it, finally I was given a break and something was working in my favor. The snow was so deep I had to walk in the street.

I slipped and fell on the wet ground in the ice and slush. I didn't even noticed both legs of my pants were socking wet with snow clinging to the bottom until I was finished replacing the tires. I was over joyed. I gladly drove down the street, my car wobbled its way to my mothers house, feeling as though anytime the tires would just pop off and roll down the street. I couldn't tell in the excitement of my discovery of the tires, but all the belts were broken in all three tires, two hours had passed, but I was able to make it to my mothers house, I set on the couch holding everything inside. I tried to mentally process what had just happen. I took a deep breath, leaning back on the couch sighing in relief, the meditation I learn overseas proved to be very adequate in this time of stress and uncertainty.

I still wearing my work uniform from the day before, knowing I had to be at work in five hours, I didn't move, I just sat on the couch trying to forget the day and get two hours of sleep before going to work. I didn't know what the future was going to be, the future of my marriage and more important the future of my children. I went to work that night, socks still wet from earlier in the day, stomach growling because I had not eaten since the night before. I reluctantly pulled on to teh parking lot at my work location 20 minutes early so I could compose myself before going into the restaurant. No matter how hard I tried I couldn't be the same happy positive person I always was, so I set in my car on the parking lot of Popeyes chicken until I collected myself, gathering strength from restless places in my soul yet to be discovered.

I walked in the restaurant, waved at the employees and position myself in the back corner half hardly watching the patriots enter and leave with smiles plastered on their face. Carrying bags of pieces of caucus home, so they can sit and devour dead relatives of chickens in front of the TV.

I was so tired I was in a daze for 10 hours, I wasn't only tired, I was mentally tired. I watch the clock every second tic by slowly as the night drew to an end. I walked outside to my car and discovered that three of my tires were flat. There was a gas station sign flickering a half a mile down the street. I tried to drive slow on the side of the road but after a half block the tires went totally flat and falling off the rims. I called a tow truck, then walked in the snow and slush 4 miles to my mothers house. My sister Sherry grudgingly open the door, mumbling something under her breath that only made sense to her. I stomped my feet twice on the porch shaking the snow free from my boots. I sat once again on the couch and let out a sign of relief, trying not to think about tomorrow because it will surely bring its own problems.

I set awake listening to thesounds of my childhood while house fall asleep settling don for teh night on its aluminum frame, the floor boards squeaked as my sisters settled in for the night. Everyone had somewhere to be or sleep except for me, I was in the mist of turbulent times, my life spiraling out of control can I like to stop the falling. It had been two days since I had eaten, I didn't care, I was focused on buying new tires and re-establishing my life.

There were rumors Gina was back in town, but my life was so out of control I didn't want too add to my problems. I tried to stay as far away from Cindy as possible, but it wasn't long before she called my mother complaining about my abandoning her and the kids, and she didn't have a ride to work. I told my mother what Cindy had done and I wasn't going to take a chance and risk having to buy new tires again. I made arrangements with Cindy, I would take her to work and pick her up. I dropped her off at teh apartment every night for a month, the drive began to become taxing, by the time I got back to my mothers house it was 1am in teh morning. It didn't make sense for me to drive all over the city and I didn't get home until 1 AM so we changed our arrangements. I began sleeping in the front room on the floor at the apartment. I left a bag of clothes in the car, only bringing a small travel bag containing underwear, toothbrush and a change of clothes.

Things seem to be going well for a couple weeks, Cindy and I managed to sleep in the same bed, even having occasional passionless sexual encounters. I still loved her but I slept with eyes wide shut. Mornings came and went, I could tell over the course of two weeks something was bothering her, but I just couldn't put my finger on it. Anytime I tried to ask her what was wrong, she just walked into the other room, not saying a word. The one thing we did agreed on was church, but neither of us was in the mood for being preach too. We needed professional marital counseling but neither of us made more than minimum wage, every penny we had went to rent and bills or food. I was barely able to pay the rent, therefore; paying someone for advice about our life wasn't even an after thought, we just couldn't afford it.

THE EXODUS

As usual, my days were very predictable, you could have set your watch by my daily events. I get off work, drive by Cindy's job, pick her up, stop by my mother in-laws house, pick the children up then drive to the apartment. I was living an uneventful boring life for a 24-year-old young man. I was beginning to believe this was my permanent place and I didn't foresee any changes in the future. Miraculously we have been in the same roof without an incident for over a month and in the process of rediscovering one another, so I thought. I pick Cindy up from work later that evening, I made my usual rounds picking up and dropping off everyone, doing my route before arriving back at our apartment. Cindy didn't say a word the entire time, although I tried to strike up a conversation, she was non-responsive and just stared out the window, seemingly preoccupied with something else. Once we arrived at the apartment I barely had the car in park before she flung the car door open, grabbing Miya by one arm, snatching her up from the back seat. I took Michaela from the back seat and carried her in the house closing the passenger door before I went inside.

I could tell she wanted to try to start another fight so, I walk Michaela inside the apartment and say good night to Cindy at teh door, but she ask me to stay. I stood idol for a moment staring at her. I ask her.

"What's wrong with you, why you so quiet?" She looked at me teary-eyed and said.

"I just had a hard day at work that's all".

Once again I fell weak for her and I stayed the night. I took off my Gun belt, unloaded my gun and placed it high on the closet shelf. I didn't feel like arguing, instead of going to bed right away I sat on the front room floor and watched the Benny Hill show. Cindy came in the room several times interrupting the TV program by turning off the TV. I didn't know at the time she wanted attention.

I wasn't educated and I didn't have a clue what she was doing so I sat on the floor, ate my cheeseburger and watched TV until 5 o'clock in the morning. I heard rustling in the hallway, I looked up Cindy was in the closet fumbling around on the shelf near my gun. I said.

"What are you doing? " I'm just getting my Bible". Extending her hand out towards me showing me her Bible. "See" she said, before going back into the bedroom.

I got up, walked over to the closet, my gun was still secure in its holster, so I sat back down to finish watching my TV program. I finally decided to call it a night, my stomach was full for the first time in weeks because I wasn't mentally distracted by constant drama. I walked into the bedroom, Cindy was lying very still on her side with a very intense stare, she clutched her Bible in her right-hand occasionally flipping through pages even ripping out three pages and placing them on the dresser. I laid in the bed beside her fully dressed. I tried to watch her but I the sand man got teh better of me and I slowly dozed off. I was soon awaken by sounds of pans rattling in the kitchen. I wasn't disturbed because I figured she was just in the kitchen preparing breakfast for the kids so I slowly began dozing off once more. Unexpectedly I was awaken by a loud bang! I was so tired I struggle to get my focus. I vaguely her heard Cindy Call my name.

"Michael"

In a faint voice, I sprung to my feet, ran into the front room. I looked at her and said. "What are you trying to do? Why is it so smoky in here? Turn the stove off."

I rushed into the kitchen, turn the knobs on the stove but the stove wasn't on. I began choking from the smoke so I walk over to the window and tried to open it, I heard Cindy gasp for breath of air, so I turned around and in astonishment there it was. I looked behind me and my 357 Magnum was lying on the floor. Cindy gasping for air, arching her back. I quickly grabbed her and laid her on the floor, placing pillows under her feet, I knew this much from my first aid training in teh military, then I frantically ran around beating on the neighbors doors asking for someone to call an ambulance.

My heart was beating at a thousand minutes per second, the police and ambulance arrived within minutes as well as the news. I was order to sit on the apartments steps while the police detectives conducted gun powder burns on my hands and fingers and halfway up my arms with a cotton swab dipped in a clear solution. Somewhere between all the chaos I was able to call my mother to come pick up the kids. I was placed in the back of a police car, staring out the window watch as they loaded Cindy in the back of the ambulance and whisk her off to the hospital. I was taken to the downtown police headquarters and placed in a small 9 x 10 room. Carpet padding on the wall with a small metal table placed squarely in the center of the room. I was left alone in the room for what seem like an hour before a young white female detective came in the room with the a clip board, and tape recorder in hand. She asked questions in duplicate, writing on a pad, and other times using a tape recorder. I walked in the interviewing booth at nine in the morning and before I know it, it was 4 PM.

One tall gangly police Sgt. walked into the room, he looked at me and said. " Your fingerprints were all over the gun".

I squinted my eyes looking at him in total discuss.

"Of course my fingerprints are all over the gun, it's my gun," I carry it to work every day" I said.

The female detective came back into the room telling me I was free to go. I walked out into the lobby and to my surprise my entire family was their in full support, for the first time in my life I saw my entire family in one place just for me. I was still in a daze and overwhelmed by what just happened, it was as if I was standing outside of my body watching myself go through this horrific ordeal. I was driven from the police station to my mother's house by my brother in-law and my older brother Denton. Before I could arrived at my mother's house, my sister received three calls from Cindy's family threatening my life.

I didn't bat an eye. I was numb by the process I just went through. I didn't want to speak to anyone or think about anything, I didn't even know if I wanted to continue to live. I was hurt right down to my core, crippling pain took over my mind and body. I knew I would have to return to the apartment and go through the distasteful process of packing up all my furniture and relocating. 'Out of sight, out of mind'. I knew it would be impossible for me to live in that apartment again.

So with the help of my family I packed up and placed all my furniture into a storage bend. My mother and I packed up the bedroom. While going through Cindy's clothes, my mother found a suicide letter written by Cindy, explaining why she killed her self. I didn't know my mother found the letter until several days later. I tried to read it but I was still in a lot of mental pain and had trouble processing the information.

Days later I had to go through the unpleasant experience of making funeral arrangements. My mother continue her support, escorting me to the funeral home, we were direct it to a room filled with endless amounts of caskets lined in rows of 5, stretching from the front to the back of the funeral parlor. My eyes found a beautiful pink and silver casket, I had no clue how I was going to pay for the funeral. I gave the funeral director the title to my car without blinking an eye. I didn't care what it cost or how long I would have to pay on it.

I wanted her to have it. The next day I took my Cindy's clothes to the funeral home but the director said Cindy's mother purchased her a dress. The dress was a loud pink, with puffy shoulders and ruffled sleeves. In other words the dress look ridiculous, but I was so emotionally distraught I didn't have it in me to challenge her decision. Before the funeral, I gave Cindy's mother her rabbit fur coat, and her new watch I bought her for her birthday and several of her rings. The day of the funeral I sat to the right side of the casket, my friend Billy said my brother Denton ask him to sit with me in his absence, so he sat next to me and provided much-needed, tremendous moral support.

My grandmother sat in the front row with my sister Marcia. It was reassuring and made me feel better just having her in the room. As the room began to fill, my cousin excused himself saying that he had to leave to open up his karate studio. I notice most of the family members were Cindy's relatives, their must have been well over 60 of her relatives in the room. I could hear loud bolstering talking coming from the entry way toward the front of the room. I looked up and it was Cindy's brother, yelling and loud talking, putting on a show for his friends and family. He turned the corner at the end of the chairs and made his way towards my grandmother. Within seconds he was in my grandmother's face yelling and talking loudly at her. I sprung from my chair tearing across the room, before I could reach him Billy grabbed me and pulled me back down in my chair. I fought and drag Billy and his

300 pounds closer to the fight. All the sudden the sound of screeching chairs intensify as Cindy's family rushed toward the front of the funeral parlor, pinning me against the wall. I was still trying to make my way toward Robbi, burly grabbing his jacket, we tussled, occasionally slamming into the casket. The casket began to rock back and forth, I thought for sure Cindy would row out onto the floor.

My friend Enron heard the commotion and ran from the back of the funeral home with his gun high in the air, yellin.

"Get back you're not going to hurt Mikey today". I didn't have time in that moment to really appreciate what he done for me, but I know I am for ever in his debt. The police swarm the funeral parlor and forced everyone to leave. My mother was out raged by the incident, she called all my family and told them what happen. Cindy's family continued calling and threatening my life, I wasn't phase the least bit. I was totally focused on putting my wife in the ground and going on with my life. Two days after we destroyed the funeral home I bury my wife, everyone in my family that attended the burial was carrying a weapon except for myself.

My mother and step father, and brother in-law had pistols in their coat pockets. All of my sisters had knives and my older brother Rayford had a pump shot gun, two police officers were assigned to me to insure another fight would not break out. I stood silently surrounded by 50 people, but I felt so along. The preacher was praying but I couldn't hear a word he uttered. I was numb to everything around me, I felt an incredible weight in my heart, it was as if someone had pulled the plug on my life. I knew I had no time to sit and feel sorry for myself I had to keep moving, feeling sorry for myself wasn't going to take care of my children are put a roof over our heads. I tried to get back on point and focus but there seemed to be a quite storm brewing within my personal space, chaos and order at the subatomic level were at odds with one another.

For weeks I sat on the steps of my mothers patio watching my daughters play with their cousins in the backyard. All of my senses were numb, I could see them yelling and screaming, I just couldn't hear them. They were very happy, 'ephemeral' for the time being, temporarily forgetting any thoughts of their mothers death. I waited and waited for them to ask where their mother was and if she was coming home, but the question never came.

Throughout the next several weeks Enron would come by my mothers house trying to encourage me and elevate my spirits, but I was to far gone to respond. It didn't matter how often someone tried to encourage me or say kind words, my subconscious would not give my mind permission to hear their kind words. Even Sgt. first class Woods from the JROTC program called and try to lift my spirits bu I was to disconsolate.

I was lachrymose from visions of Cindy lying lifeless on the front room floor, tubes coming out of every extremity. I was on the mental journey of mortification, as penance, I chose to give up sexual relationships. I no longer gallivanted around looking for easy prey. I accepted it as a form of retribution, my predilection for huge breasts and long brown legs have all but mentally disappeared. I had to travel this role of discontent and despair all by myself, this wasn't a jaunt venture, I was trying to live a peripatetic life. I had to change how I lived because until now every bad decision I made had a female accelerant.

When Someone commit suicide, not only does it kill that person, it damages everything in its path, it disrupts life by creating unsuspecting battles of blame and fault between the survivors.

(Whip Rawlings)

Sgt. Walt thought it best that I go right back to work rather than sit around thinking about my wife's death, therefore; three days after she was placed in the ground I was back at work, carrying a new 38 pistol issued to me by my security agency until I could afford to purchase a new gun. Because I carried a firearm I was placed in some of the most economically depressed areas in Indianapolis. I worked in these arrears before, but under my current mental status I was in no mood to arrest or handcuff anyone, in fact I didn't even load my gun. There was a time I would have made three arrest in one day, but now I just stood in the food freezer and watch the local kids steal the store blind. I knew I was not doing anyone any good so I requested to work 12 hour shifts on the highway, putting batteries in the yellow blinking lights, directing traffic away from the construction zone. I found myself working in a small town on the outskirts of Indianapolis, I didn't know the town exist until I started working in that particular location.

I carried a six pack of beer on the front seat and a nickel bag of marijuana to help me get the ghost out of my head. It worked for a short while but once the high was gone, pain rushed my body like someone had lit a match to my soul. I parked behind the construction barriers and chuck rocks at the cows on the other side of the fence. I got lost in space and time watching the cows eat their cut of grass, while I smoked my grass.

I never liked marijuana, it made my head feel weird, and my eyes burn. I got so hungry I left my post and ran to McDonald's every 15 minutes, but I didn't have a choice, my mind was clogged with thoughts of the morning of March 29, questioning whether I could have done something different that would have prevented this tragedy or was I predestined to travel this road. As they say in the Marine Corps I didn't know whether I was 'shot, fucked, powder burned or snake bite'. I was going down shit creek without a paddle. There were organizations that could have helped me but I wasn't aware of any of those resources. I was a very private person and told my business to no one. I was also too proud to ask for help, I like to handle things on my own with as little interference from the public as possible. My greatest fortune was, my mother had the foresight to see that I needed space and time to recover, so she stepped in and took charge of my girls which gave me a chance to breath, catch my breath and regroup.

THE BIBLE LESSON

I work two minimum wage jobs, trying to fill the empty space in my head. Making such low wages I was forced to move into a shabby run down studio apartment on 38th and Emerson, my two girls lived with my mother, giving me time to collect myself and recuperate. The apartment was small. It couldn't have been more than 200 Ft.² in the whole apartment, with just a front room and a bathroom. I didn't care about the condition of the apartment because I was never home for more than an hour at a time if I wasn't sleeping. I worked two jobs to ensure that I was mentally occupied for most of my working hours of the day. My working hours I ran back to back, one job so that I could pay child support and the other job so that I could support myself and my girls. I worked non-stop with a two hour break between jobs, with just enough time to change from one uniform to the other.

Each job required me to be constantly on my feet for 12 hours or more. I walked through the grocery stores on one job and on my other job I walked the hallways of a Very ritzy apartment complex. I patrolled the complex half asleep and physically wiped out. Cindy was hunting me from within. I couldn't escape thoughts of her in my head, my mind raced constantly plunging me deeper into depression. I work six days a week mostly 12 hour shifts with Sundays off each week. I spent most of my free time tinkering around with my car, ensuring the maintenance was up to date. Occasionally I would see a tall woman walking past my car clutching her Bible to her bosom. Her dress hung slightly pass her knees, she gave me a broken smile, never saiding a word as she went up the steps into her apartment. Sunday after Sunday she walked pass, this time she waved, acknowledging my presents, she smiled at me then into our apartment building she went, not saying a word.

One day I was repairing a broken center length on the bottom front of my car, in an instance a shadow was blocking the sun, I stuck my head from under the car to see what had eclipsed the sunlight. I stared up and there were two long unshaved legs standing right over my head. I polity turned my head to the side, trying not to disrespect her by looking up her dress.

I said, "Can I help you?"

She said, "When are you coming to church with me?"

She stood their clutching her Bible, wearing a high collar silk blouse, hair tied to the top of her head as if she was a secretary. She wasn't very attractive, but she seemed genuine and religious. I didn't feel threaten by her because I was in no mental position to date anyone.

I ignored her and continued to work on my car. She said, "Alright"

And back up the stairs she went. Every Sunday she would stop by and invite me to come to church with her, and every Sunday I refused. I was still angry at God for allowing Cindy to take herself away from her children, so I denied her based on the fact that I worked six days a week and didn't want to spend my only day off work listening to a preacher. After three months of her asking me to attend church, I caved in like a cake in the oven. Sunday school began at 8: am I was dead on my feet because I worked the grave yard shift at Morrat apartments until 7: am. After four hours of church I was ready for bed, but she wanted to continue on with the bible lesson. Once we arrived back at the apartment she invited me up stairs for more Bible study. I told her I was tired but she was relentless and insisted I come up stairs.

She said, "Come up in 15 minutes".

So I went into my apartment and change into sweat pants, grabbed my Bible and a pad of paper then headed up stairs. I noticed her apartment door was slightly ajared, so I knocked on the door.

"Come in and have a se, I'm in the tub". She said, yelling from the bathroom.

I step inside and looked to my right, there she was sitting in the bathtub with the door partially opened just enough for me to see that she was in the tub. I thought nothing of it, so I sat quitely on her couch until she finish bathing. I could hear her drying off and the water draining from the tub. She yelled from the bathroom.

"Close your eyes I'm coming out".

She wrapped a small white towel around her body, hanging just an eighth of an inch below her pelvic area, as she quickly walked into her walk-in closet. I sat on the couch thumbing through my Bible waiting for the Bible lesson to begin, all at once she emerged from the closet wearing a black see through gown. She struted back and forth across the room, purposely stopping in the light reflecting through the window to feed my sexual appetite. I didn't know what to think, 'was she trying to seduce me into sex'? Or did she really not know I can see through her gown when she stood by the window in the light, it really didn't matter because I was brain dead and emotionally drained at the moment.

I was damage goods, sex was the farthest thought from my mind, for the first time in my life I didn't recognize a sexually opportunity placed right in my face. I sat idoly on the couch turning the pages of my Bible waiting for the Bible lesson that never came. Eventually I headed down stairs leaving her sexually aroused and wanting, as I reach the stair case I heard the door slam behind me in sexual fraustation. I returned to my apartment disappointed because I didn't receive my Bible lesson. I opended the door to my dark cold apartment and fell face down on my sofa bed. I was so tired I was asleep before my head firmly touch the pillow and for the first time in two months Cindy's ghost didn't have room to run free in my head. I woke up six hour later, shower and started to get dressed for work. I sat in the chair next to the window bending over tieing my shoes and that was the last thing I remember. I fell asleep sitting up, tieing my shoes. I was an hour late for work that day, my uniform was neatly pressed, my gun was empty but my mind was full.

The same voice played over and over in my head like a broken record. "She just check out" "she just checked out" "she just checked out leaving our two girls". I couldn't get the voices out of my head so for the next several months I worked non-stop, day and night until I dropped from exhaustion or had no room in my head for thoughts of Cindy, but it didn't work. So I hit the night clubs in between shifts, trying to find comfort in a bottle of liquor. With two half pints of Winsor canadan, one in each pocket, that wasn't good enough, so I purchased two cans of beer, mixing beer and wine all night until I couldn't walk. The irony of the whole drinking event was, I didn't like alcohol. I couldn't stand the taste of it, but I wasn't drinking for enjoyment, I was drinking to get wasted.

I got so drunk I was carried to the door by a co-worker from the grocery store, he pointed me in the direction of my car then shoved me toward the parking lot. I slowly walked, sliping and sliding my way to my car. Ice crumbling beneath my feet and the wind cut through my suit like razor blades. Ice covering the windows and doors prevented me from entering my car quickly, first I drunkenly chip the ice from the key hold and forced the door open separting the ice from the door hang. I flopped down lifelessly onto the drivers seat and tossed my keys under the front seat. Within seconds I passed out.

I was awaken four hours later by tapping on my window, someone was asking if I was ok, in that instance my fingers began to burn as if they were frost bitten, for a moment I thought I was back in Korea doing Jack Frost training. I frantically began seaching for my keys, after several minutes of searching I located my keys and managed to start the car. My fingers were stinging badly, I couldn't even make a fist, but somehow I did get my car started. I jumped on the highway heading for home, going 5 miles per hour the entire way. I barely noticed the other cars blowing their horns and flashing their headlights as I creped down the highway swaying back and forth crossing several lines before exiting the highway on Emerson.

I knew I couldn't continue this pace, my life was flashing before my eyes, it seemed nothing I tried was working. I worked two security jobs, one job required that I carry a weapon. I may just enough money to pay child support and a few of my bills. I couldn't even make payments on the funeral. Cindy laid in Hill Cemetery in a unmarked grave. I couldn't focus on that for the moment, I had to focus on the living. I had to focus on raising my daughters, everything else is secondary. I needed college but at this time it wasn't an option, I wasn't groom for college as a child and even if I had been groom for college I would have failed in the process due to my current mental state.

ARMED BUT NOT SO DANGEROUS

Before the weekend I received my new work schedule and to my surprise someone assigned me to work at the grocery store two blocks from Cindy's brothers house located in a low income part of Indianapolis. It was very typical for an armed guard to be placed in dangerous locations even though I knew how to communicate with people, this location was a double threat so I had to be really careful and stay out of harms way but I also knew Murphy's law. If something can go wrong it will go wrong. One day Murphy's Law showed up. As usual I was in my depressed mood, lost in thought and everyone knew it. They knew I wasn't the same man working in their grocery store two months earlier. I had changed and they could see it was a dramatic change. I no longer felt compelled to arrest anyone. I hardly pay attention to patriots walking in the store, but one day two men walked into the store and position themselves on each side of the door. I automatically knew something was wrong, we stirred at each other until the store manager signal me over.

He said. "These two men robbed the store the year before", "the men made us all get undress and lay down on the floor".

After hearing this news my heart began to beat faster, my palms were sweaty. I knew my gun was not loaded so, I maded my way to the back of the store then slipped behind a two-way mirror located behind the meat department. I loaded my gun then went out the opposite end of the storage room, out of the view of the store mirrors. I watch the two men in the mirrors as I slowly walked back to the front of the store. I left the strap to my gun holster unfastened and leaned back against the grocery carts with my right hand slung over the trigger my weapon. The two men staired at me very intensely, I believe they thought they could punk me and made me back down, but if they only knew what I had just gone through they would've hastily left the store without a hitch.

But that wasn't the case, so we staired intensely at one another burley bating an eye. The stair off went on for 5 more minutes, we were frozen in time, in dead silence, you could hear a pin hit the floor. The two men began to breathe heavy, they looked at each other then quickly stuck their hands down the inside their coats, at that moment I fully gripped my gun with my finger resting alongside the trigger guard.

Just as I reclined a little more against the grocery carts, the carts began to roll back causing me to lose my balance and fall toward the ground. The two men seize the opportunity and began to pull their hands out of their coats, at the same time as I was falling back on the grocery carts. I drew my gun from it's holster, simultaneously cocking the trigger back as the gun begins to level in their direction, the two men threw their hands in the air and yelled.

"Ok man, were gone".

Then ran from the store. That incident was a sobering assessment of reality, I knew I could no longer walk around in a daze and put my life on the line for pennies. I had more to be concerned about than myself or just making a living. I was placing my life and my children's future in jeopardy. I felt overwhelmed with life, I couldn't see a way out, if I didn't know any better I would have thought the moon was in my fifth Solar house. I felt trapped, here I was working in a low income dangerous job with no future prospects, not even health and dental insurance or life insurance. I was making just enough money to survive. This ideal of feeling trapped kept me up for nights, pacing the floor and staring out the window wondering about the future of my children.

By this time Gina was trying to reenter my life, I started out just watching my son while she went to work, then occasionally she would come over with her favorite meal, cold cuts and chips with a 2 ounce bottle of Pepsi to wash it all down. We sat on my sofa bed, ate lunch and talk about nothing, trying to reestablish a relationship that would never come into fruition. Love was lost because I had an anger brewing inside of me for her that burned hotter than fire. I was told by family members a few weeks after Cindy passed away, that Gina was calling her on her job and telling her she was going to make me marry her because she was pregnant with my child. It was hard to believe she did all of those things, I just couldn't see that in her spirit. I was totally disappointed in her and could barely look at her without my eyes watering from rage and disappointment.

I just didn't believe she would do that but I was wrong and I promise myself it will be the last time I would be wrong about a woman's personality. I was to trust no one and feel nothing for anyone, I was just going to go through the motions, leaving broken hearts on a tearless path. There was no time for tears, I had to make a shift in my life but I didn't know where I was going or how I will get their, but I knew I had to do something even if it was drastic. I needed a third income, so I decided to take the exam for the Marine Corps reserves, then a light bulb came on in my head, therefore; I returned to Active duty in the Marines and was promptly sent back to Camp Pendleton within a week. Traditionally Marines don't allow single parents with children to serve, but I had an ace in my pocket. May had been after me for sometime to marry her but I wasn't ready at the time but now I was without a choice. She knew my kids very well and they appear to be emotionally attached to her.

I have known May and her family for most my life, so I decided to married my high school sweet heart, our first attempt at marriage fell by the wayside, with all the uncertainty around me I wasn't sure if I could go through with it, therefore; I didn't show up the day we were supposed to go to The justice of peace. May was thoroughly pissed off and refused to have sex with me.

She said. "I'm saving myself for my husband".

I just couldn't bring myself to do it, it had only been 12 months since my wife passed away and I just wasn't ready for another commitment but every time I looked at my girls I grow weaker. I knew they needed a female presences in their life, someone I can trust, someone that I've known for a long time, someone with some measure of integrity. I decided to move forward with the marriage. The next day May wrapped her arm around my arm then escorted me downtown to the justice of peace. The court personnel ask.

"When do you want to get married?" "Right now!" May said, in an authoritative voice.

She wouldn't let me out of her sight for one-second until the vowels were read and we exchanged rings. I was still feeling the wrath from my first marriage, I wasn't certain if I could consummate our marriage.

May went into the bathroom to get ready and I set on the couch trying to remove the tension from around my eyes. After she finished taking a shower I went to the bathroom, once she laid on the big orange pillow waiting for our first night of marital bliss. I stalled in the bathroom taking a long shower than usual, trying to psych myself up for night of passion and unbridle sex. Little did she know I wasn't in the mood. I was put off by the ideal of her being my latest mistake.

"What did I just do?"

I ask myself over and over trying to find a moment of clarity about the shackles of love I once again signed up for. I was still bleeding inside from the mortal wounds of my first marriage. I knew I couldn't love her fully at the moment because I couldn't love myself. She laid ready waiting on a large orange pillow in the center of the room for our first attempt at making a child. I was just a shell of the person in bed I once was, I no longer care that she had a perfect set of 36 double D's that made me crumble to my knees just from the excitement of seeing them. I was still mentally traumatized by the events of my first marriage. I stayed awake that night staring out the window as May slept quietly on the large orange pillow. I stay awake watching the nights walkers come out while all the working stiffs prepared for a night of rest.

ONCE A MARINE

I was full of excitement and anticipation at the posibility of seeing old friends. I had just re-enlisted in the Marine Corps, something I never thought I would do again, after my first enlistment I thought I was surely finished with the Corp, with banging my knees up, freezing half to death in 30° below zero weather, running up mountains and going on 24.3 mile forest Marches with full gear. Re-enlisting in the corp was the only choice that made since at the time. Four years would give me time to clear my head and collect my thoughts and make an effective plan for my kids and myself. I was truly a single parent now, life had converted into to a game of chess and I was new to the game. I had no time for tears. I had to think five years ahead because every move dictated how I would live years from now. I was playing for keeps, age was caughting up with me. I had a wife and three kids with one on the way. Every move I made at this point in my life was financially critical. I never thought in my wildest dreams I would be married to someone who didn't want to work or work as a team to secure our financial independence. But that was the reality, she didn't want to work and it was all left up to me.

    I understood clearly I was passed my prime for taking orders or putting up with anyones non- since. The Corp was full of people that love to usurp their authority or play head games, such as washing trucks while it's raining, cleaning weapons all day, are performing drill from sun rise to taps. The only good thing about re-enlisting was I didn't have to go to boot camp again. If I was aware of other options I would'nt have re-enlisted in the Marine Corps. As a yound adult I was never groomed for college, so the thought of going to college or a trade school never enter into my mind. Jobs were difficult to fine. Most days, lent filled my pockets in places money should've been. Trying to support 3 kids on minimum wage wasn't an easy task. I often found myself short changed, just a enough money to pay my bills and buy food, I struggle horribly.

I needed a break, I needed to go where I could make a decent income and not worry about where my next meal is coming from.

The Marines are a tough outfit and because I was a little older I was uncertain weather I could keep up with the excruciating fast pace the Marines demanded. Had to get my life started again so I requested to be shipped out as soon as possible so that I could get situated before my family arrived.

my first task was to find an apartment near my base, Camp Pendleton. Finding an apartment within my income range was no an easy task, but other marines were living near the base, I just followed their lead. I needed an apartment less than 10 miles from the base entrance, because my camp was another 10 miles inside the base down a long dark winding road, full of cougars, Bob cats, Snakes and Coyotes. The base was a wild life preservation.

Cindy's spirit followed us right into the military, walking around the new apartment, peeking out of closets at our children and occasionally scaring May half to out of head. This marriage wasn't too bad, I thought, she's didn't pull knives out on me and her moments of anger could be defused with an evening out to dinner or a small gift. After five months of marriage I began to open up just a little, but I was being sexually deprived, never feeling comfortable enough to express myself sexuality freely. We were having sex three times a week and I was beginning to develop some feelings for her but deep down inside my murky subconscious I was screaming

"No! Don't trust it".

I ignored the voices in my head because I want this marriage to work. I was willing to put every part of myself into it even if it meant I had to put my feelings on hold and bend over backward further than I ever had for anyone. I was willing to do it because I want to stay married. I started off right away practicing what I preached, I stayed home, I didn't talk to or chase other women. I spent most of my recreation time running 5 miles a day or watching the local stations on our cable less TV.

I was with my family seven days a week, except for the times I'd deploy overseas to training. We spent the next five months getting to know one another's faults and the things we enjoy. I enjoyed watching her get out of the tub soaking wet and she enjoyed when I took her places and brought her things. I quickly learned she had two deal breaker faults. The first fault was she didn't know how to cook, I knew it was common for many first-time wives to lack in their ability to cook so I ignored it and pretend to like whatever she prepared, such as the overcooked pork chops, shrink down to the size of a silver dollar, it was like eating leather without seasoning. Ravioli, fresh out of the can was the other main course I suffered through weekly.

I didn't even complain about her famous meat loaf which taste like cardboard with ketchup poured over it. Her second and greatest fault, she didn't pro form oral sex on me, she loved to have it performed on her but she didn't return the favor. Our sex life was very basic, no experimenting in the bedroom, and there was no element of surprise to our love making. She did nothing to make me want her or want to be around her. I knew the exact date, hour and minute we were going to have sex and it drove me crazy. I was bored out of my mind. I'm a Sagittarius and everyone knows Sagittarius are some of the freakiest lovers on the planet, the one thing we hate more then anything else is boring sex.

Within 6 to 7 months of being married she achieved her ultimate goal, she was pregnant and I must say her skin was as smooth and healthy looking as I have ever seen it. But her insides were turning into something sadistic and evil, she plotted her escape from our marriage day by day, week by week and month by month, decisively and secretively setting money aside in a separate account unknown to myself. Very often She complained about not having enough money but she set around the house watching TV, constantly refusing to work or offer any help with our financial situation, however I did respect her ability to save money but she wasn't very overt and inclusive with the money she squirreled away. After having our daughter she changed her personality like a burnt out lite bulb, the secluded things she did where no longer hidden, they were up close and in my face. She became cold and withdrawn, not wanting to have sex, or sleep in the same bed because she felt I wanted anytime she brushed against me in bed. She spent every waking hour poisoning my daughter mind by whispering negative thoughts in her virgin ears.

By the time she was 18 months old she wouldn't come with a foot of me, I believe I lost her, never having a chance to bond with her. I was shut out from having any relationship with my daughter. Her mother carried her around the house continuously clutched in her arms, not letting her out of her sight more than a second. I was systematically being removed from my daughters life with hate and lies. During the 36 months we spent in Hawaii , she made my life pure hell, not wanting to cook, and being unaffectionate. She never tried to communicate what was bothering her, she just shut down and build a invisible wall around herself and my daughter that felt very real. Our sexual life was cut down to one day a week, just on Saturdays which meant we had a sexless marriage. I did not understand at first but I quickly learned that controlling sex was her way of having power and having control over something in our marriage. I tried everything to make our marriage work, but she became more distance and harder to please.

After being on the island for 18 months my unit was being rotated overseas to Okinawa Japan on a six month deployment. I couldn't help but notice May seemed all to happy that I was going away, I spent most of the day packing my gear, she walked back and forth pass the bedroom, smelling every time I packed a jacket or a pair of pants. I was truly hoping we could spend four hours making love before I departed for the bus, but she waited until the last 30 minutes before my departure before offering herself up for sex. As boring as our sexual experience was, I couldn't turn it down. I would be without sex for six months, so I obliged her for our usual 10 minutes worth of unpassionate sex.

I toss my seabag in the back of the car then ran back in the house for one last swallow of Kool- Aid. I couldn't help but notice my half pint of peppermint snaps was three quarters gone. May lead a very secretive life when I wasn't around, she drank liquor and smoke cigarettes but never in my presence. She was very good at making me believe she was someone other than whom she presented herself to be. We rode quietly to the staging area, I remove my bags from the car and got one last unaffectionate kiss before boarding the bus.

I was on my way to Japan once again where sexual pleasure was $15 for 15 minutes and a five minute cab ride to town, but had grew in he last two years, I was a different person with different desires and needs. I didn't see the geisha girls in the same light as I once did. I no longer cared about the banana shows or having women set on my lap half dressed while I bought them water down drinks with the purpose of securing a night in their bed. During my first three months in Japan I spent most of the time penniless. I wrote letter after letter to May requesting that she sent me enough money to maintain my uniforms but there was no reply, I had to borrow money from my friends or work their shift as duty NCO for the night. I charged twenty-five dollars to take their shift while they ran wild in the streets of Japan. Being station in Japan without money was like going to Vegas just to see the lights and watch everyone else gamble and have fun.

There was so many things I wanted to buy for my children and my wife. Not having money left me restricted to the barracks and the base gym. Lucky for me my roommate rented a television for entertainment so I stayed in my room and watched movies most of the weekend. I didn't need money for food but a special treat once in a while would have helped me get through the six months. I was confined too eating mid Rations handed out at the chow hall at 10 PM. Everyone else was going to town shopping and having fun, I watched as the honcho's (taxi cab) pulled away from the curb heading to BC Street or Gate Two. Okinawa was not unfamiliar to me because I lived on the island in 1980 during my youth as a young Lance Corporal.

I had experienced the island years before most of the men in my unit had joined the military, however; that didn't stop me from poking my head inside the hotels catching the site of a couple of beautiful Asian women. One thing I didn't have to worry about was fornication because I didn't have much money and the small amount of money I did have I wasn't going to wasted on women. Before I knew it I was boarding a ship on my way to South Korea, a place I thought I would never see again. Orders came down that we were to do a beach assault, it wasn't my first time so I didn't think twice about it, but the other young Marines were apprehensive about riding in a U-boat. They all heard stories of the enormous waves slamming aganist the boat, soaking the entire crew from head to toe. We set out at 4 AM a.m. in the morning wearing flag jackets and carrying our rifles. I thought it odd that we weren't taking our cannons with us. We rode around aimlessly on the ocean for two hours. Huge waves crashed on to the side of U- boats nearly drowning us as we held onto the rails.

"Abandon ship!" Yelled the U-boat Driver.

I thought he had made a mistake, I looked around the boat for holes but the U-boat appear to be intact.

"Over the side, now!"

He yelled with a more forceful voice. The sides were too high for us to jump over, so one man squatted down while the others stepped on his back to jump over the side into the freezing waters. I was the first to jump over the side, trying to set an example for the younger marines..

Heavy ocean waves slammed against me as I fell head first into the ocean, sinking 5 feet then returning instantly to the surface. It took less than 10 minutes to empty the six U-boats. My first sergeant stood atop a boat yelling instructions for us to lock arms. The waves were unforgiving, we were being slapped around like a rubber duck in a bathtub. I was one of the strong swimmers, so I was given the task of bring in all the stragglers and connecting them to the rest of the line.

The line lasted about 10 minutes, every time a huge wave came crashing down on top of us taking us under water for more than a second, someone would panic and break free of the chain. We spent three hours in the water that afternoon being slam and swallowed up by huge waves. I thought for sure I would get hypothermia if we stayed in the water any longer. I was shaking so bad from the ice cold water my arms almost let loose several times as I rejoin the group after rounding up stragglers. We played in the water until we successfully broke the chain and reform again and again without breaking the chain due to the massive waves slamming against our platoon. To add insult to injury it took twice as long to get back in the U-boat as it did to get out. Icy water drained from our uniforms as we pulled back into the whale deck of the ship five hours after we left, my eyelids were all but frozen to the top of my head.

My ears were red and burning, my fingers were dysfunctional. I couldn't even unbutton my shirt to get undress. Everyone's shook like branches on a tree hurrying to relieve ourselves of the below zero clothing we were wearing. I ask myself the question once again.

"What the hell am I doing here?"

Although I just got my first taste of freezing Korean Ocean waters, Korea was much more pleasant this time, we arrived in the beginning of the spring. The temperature was around 40° much better than my first time in Korea during Jack frost training were the temperature was -30 degrees.

After a change of clothes our unit was directed to to a familiar place. The DMZ, we went straight out to the field, my fingers and ears have yet to return to a normal state from the freezing ocean water.

We traveled up and down the concave slopes of South Korea, the countryside was beautiful, their were rice patties as far as the I can see. Captain Head woke us up at four in the morning just for harassment. He made us do jumping jacks, sit ups and push ups on the ice cold rice patties. He stood on top of a hill polluting the air with his stogie cigar, 'a want to be general' smiling to himself. We were told to get a quick cold shave before going to chow. Everyone saluted the Capt. as they walk past, but I knew better. You weren't supposed to salute an officer in the field so I abide by the rules and walked right pass the captain not even pretending to like or respect him by giving him a salute. The first sergeant reached over to stop me but the captain said let him go it's okay. I didn't think anything of that incident for the moment but it would come back to haunt me a couple of months later.

I show the young Marines how to negotiate with the Koreans, trading their MRE's for Ramen noodle and a soda. Before pulling out I was told to take my gun section and patrol 5 miles out. I was given coordinates on a map and a compass. I was the highest ranking member in my section so I was put in charge of a 9 squad man. I put the young man in line formation then asked the Korean soldier where the restrooms were, he pointed towards the top of the hill. I sprinted up the hill towards the bathroom stretching open the door, I looked around and there was no toilets, it was just a big open empty room. I close the door and ran back down the hill. I ask the Korean soldier.

"Where is the restroom?, that's just an empty building". The soldier said, "Lift up the board on the floor".

I ran back up the hill and did as he instructed, there was a bottomless pit of a hole in the floor, the hole was saturated with liquefy feces, "Not again" I thought to myself, this reminded me of the bathrooms in 1980 during our Jack's frost training.

I got fully undressed pinched a loaf, then went on patrol with my man. We patrol 5 miles out checking the area for high explosives or North Koreans along the DMZ. We came across hundreds of dirt mounds with three course meals on plates at the foot of the mounds, we couldn't read the signs but somehow we knew they were Graves. Koreans were known for burying the family in the upright sitting position. I found the tradition to be strange but nevertheless I respected their burials and instructed my man to do as well. In the distance I could see a huge bundle of wood going up the side of the mountain, the wood was at least stack 20 feet high, it seemed to move on its own, but the closer we got we could see there was a little old lady carrying all that wood, she had amazing strength.

We spent our day patrolling through their neighborhoods as occupying forces. I never felt so embarrassed as an American. I knew in my heart the United States would never tolerate an occupying force patrolling their neighborhoods, what we were doing was wrong and I felt the worse for it.

The young Marines were impressed with my map reading skills and my ability to use a compass. I wish my commanders felt the same way. It wasn't in my DNA to kiss up to anyone, I was going to make rank for doing an excellent job, not for shining the captains boots with my lips. We return to Okinawa six weeks later and I was excited about the possibility of being promoted to Sgt. There was one opening left for the rank of Sgt. I wasn't worried, my only competition was a shit bird Cpl. from Canon number five with a very bad attitude, his uniform was wrinkled, his face was unshaved and his booths were never polished. I knew when they selected one of us for the promotion I would win by a landslide. I stood in formation anticipating to be called forward to have my sergeant stripes pinned on.

The First sergeant called the unit to attention then called Cpl. ving to the front of the formation, as he read the promotion order, I couldn't contain myself. I stepped out of the formation and walk away. No one said a thing, not even my Captain, as I walked back to the barracks, steam billowing from my ears with total disappointment on my face. I work so hard the last two years trying to prove I was a good leader but they gave my stripes to someone that was unworthy of it just to make a point. I didn't care what they did to me at that point I was done with the Marine Corps. I had approximately 2 years left to serve. And if it weren't for my family I would have gotten myself put in the Brig for disobeying orders. I knew I had to get the captain back for passing me over, I wanted to frag him but I had no means to carry out the ordeal so I placed it in the back of my mind for the moment.

All the sudden Japan got colder, I was no longer performing extra duties for my troops. I laid back and let the new sergeant assume his position, in my mind it was sink or swim. I wasn't going to carry him, he would have to do it on his own. I stop talking to everyone for a while I had nothing else to say at the moment, I set in my barracks and read magazines, occasionally staring out the window watching the honchos lined up below the USO club, waiting to whisk young Marines to town. I envied the young Marines freedom and single life status, most of the young Marines admired my married life, how I spend time with my family, going to the beach on week ends and walking around the base at night, but they were looking from the outside in. I was living in the corner of perception reality. Every thing they thought they knew about my marriage, they were wrong, there were rumors that one of the sergeants saw my wife in the NCO club with another man. I was married to a women that only showed love when she had a pocket full of dead presidents or when everything was perfect for her.

The months passed at a snells pace, the financial purse strings were under her control, money was a commodity unfamiliar to myself. No money came from home, not even a letter explaining why. I wrote home continuously and still there was no answer. Finally a small envelope arrived with $180.00 dollars wrapped in foil. Even though it was a small portion of my income i was glad to have it. most of the money went to paying off people I'd borrowed from, the rest was used to maintain my uniforms and for hair cuts. My base salary was 1700 dollars a month after taxes; my wife was keeping well over 1600 dollars to herself, we lived in base housing , therefore our rent was automatically deducted from my pay. There was no reason for her not to send me money more often.

During the last two months of my tour of duty in Japan I got another letter. I noticed the envelope was stamped with an Indianapolis post mark showing that the envelope was coming from Indianapolis. My emotions shifted, suddenly her motives were clear, I could feel the strings of my heart being tugged across the vast ocean to my hometown 'Indianapolis'. I was immediately incensed and outraged, there was nothing I could do, I had power of nothing, it was obvious my wife had left me and returned home, 'to Indianapolis'. I spent my last two months on the edge of my seat, trying not to think of the reason for her exodus, she could have done anything she wanted, but she chose to set around the house drinking liquor, smoking cigarettes. Instead of going out getting what she wanted she laid around the house complaining about what she didn't have.

The six month tour of duty had run its course, my unit rotated back to Hawaii just in time for tourist season on the Hawaiian Islands. As the bus enter the base gate I noticed wife's of other marine's standing on the side walk waiting for their husbands. I didn't bother to look around for a ride home, I knew my wife wasn't there. I walked six blocks home to a dark empty house, the grass was over grown, spiders webs cover the front pouch and warning letters from the base housing authority were plastered all over the front and back door, our new 1987 Mazda 626 was covered with rust and cob webs because the car and the house went unattended for more than a month. I could see the early signs that this marriage was dis functional and not going to work, she wasn't strong enough to be a military wife or loving enough to share a life with anyone a wife.

She blamed me for everything that went wrong in the marriage but little did she know it takes two people willing to move forward in the right direction and build on the relationship. My misfortune of burying my first wife just three years earlier left me tender hearted and sensitive, just the thought of her death made my throat tighten and my eyes water.i was open for interpretation of how should work. Weaken by my circumstances I allowed her to be the fore runner in our marriage. I bent over backwards allowing her room to grow, removing myself from the presence of others narrowing and refining my focus toward my family. I was emotionally invested my new unsolicited form of bondage, but my emotions were mixed between two women, my first marriage and the women I was currently married too. My first was emotionally unstable but she knew how to love. With this wife everything was on purpose, including her distance unpleasent attitude, but I was willing to allow her latitude. Leting her operate at her own pace, leaning to her own understanding.

I hated failure and I wasn't going to see my marriage fail. I believed it was all just a misunderstanding, a lack of communication and we could work it out. I made several attempts to reach May over the phone but no answer. After one week of calling she finally answered her phone.

I Asked, "What are you doing in Indianapolis?" "and are you coming back home"? She said, "No, I'm not, I'm staying here".

I she didn't have to say another word. I was done with her insidious and ridiculous BS, I slammed the phone down, rip the phone cord out of the wall, tossing the phone on the couch. I couldn't believe her arrogant and unappreciated of attitude, she practically begged me to marry her, but now that she has a legitimate child through marriage and a possible means of guranteed child support through the military, she wanted to run off and keep the child all to herself. She had me confused with someone else, I wasn't much for sitting around and crying over spilled milk, besides I had reached my limited of indifference.

I sat on the couch for a moment trying to collect myself, jumping to my feet I step into the shower, washing all the bad aura out of my personal space. I got dressed in casual clothing and hit the night clubs. One of my friends Sgt. Mallory and I headed for Hick com Air force base, where women were sure to out number the men two to one in the NCO club where Marines were not allowed entry unless they were E-5 or above. Mallory drove that night, as it turned out, it was fortunate for me.

Once in the club, I scoped the bar with dishonorable intentions in mind, I took my seat in the stands as far away from the crowd as possible. I couldn't help but noticed a Filipino women with long hair stretching down beyond our waistline, seating by herself. With my drink in one hand I approach her and asked if I could set with her, she said that her date was getting her a drink. Several minutes when by and he still hasn't returned with their drinks. I took a detour by the bar to check out the competition, there he was with two young attractive women.

I ran back to the table and pointed at her boyfriend, ensuring she saw the two well equipped young girls that he was hoping to seduce, giving him younger options. She moved down by the bar to get a better look at romeo in action, then returned to me and asked if could show her how to get off the base. I was all to glad to help. I hurry her out of the club to the car so fast she tripped and fell grabbing my crotch on the way down. I was able to catch her before she hit the pavement. We disappeared off the base like a Fantom in the night before he knew she was gone. We jumped in the car and drove to downtown Honolulu and parked at the tennis courts on Waikiki Blvd. We talked for several minutes enagaing in idol conversation until my beer went flat. I offered to drive us to the nearest liquor store but,

She said, "There's no need".

She she turn the key, her trunk flung open like a Jack in the box. Her trunk was an argosy of several types of liquor, beer nuts, chips and ice. I couldn't believe my eyes, she had everything in her trunk that a local bar would have. We sat in front of the tennis courts until 3 AM in the morning drinking mixed drinks and smoking cigarettes, keeping up idle conversations as the liquor and steal smell of cigarettes brought us closer to what we both secretly knew was going to happen, 'unbridle sex', a one night stand absent of love. I had no feelings for her, I didn't love her or cared if I ever saw her again. I didn't even remember her name. I just wanted a quickie. I wasn't trying to fall in love, I didn't want her phone number, I just needed quick relief after six months of abstinence. The one night stand turned in to three months.

It seemed every waken moment I was conscious we were having sex, it didn't matter where or what time of the day, she wanted it all the time. We went to a bar just about every night, never entering the bar, just sitting on the parking lot and drinking our own liquor from the trunk of her car as she chain smoked cigarettes and told me about her future plans. After several minutes of downing drinks, she climbed into the back seat and disrobe, she was always very demonstrative, stretching spread eagle across the seat with one leg on the back seat head rest and the other between the front seat stroking my side with her foot provoking me into action. I Watched her from my rear view mirror, she took deep drags from her cigarette while seductively rubbing her hands between her thighs inviting me to climb to the back, for the second time in my life I just wanted to sit and talk, but I thought to myself "what the hell" so I disrobed, jumped into the back seat and rode her hard until the mosquitoes got the best of both of us.

We hanged out just about every night, mostly just drinking from the ready-made bar in the truck of her car, talking about future plans and having unbridle sex. It was a nice break and change of pace from the stalemate marital position I was currently in. I didn't like being unfaithful to my wife but she was forcing me out to the streets, and nightclubs due to her unaffectionate ways and her poor attitude of what she believes a wives roll is supposed to be. I was tired of adjusting myself to fit her attitude, I was tired of coming home to meals that weren't fit for human consumption. I was tired of the sexless nights and sleeping alone. I was just sick and tired of being sick and tired.

For the first time in my life someone had more stamina then I. Threee months in to our relationship she began to fall in love, after every sexual encounter, she placed $40 dollars in my pocket and told me to go have breakfast. I didn't think much of it the first time it happen, but after each time we had sex she continued her practice of putting $40 in my pocket. I was beginning to take offense to it so I handed her back the money.

She said, "No, you keep it, go have breakfast".

I said, "Wait a minute, I'm beginning to feel like a fucking prostitute, I don't want your money, you don't have to pay me, I like you anyway".

This went on for several weeks and the ideal of taking money for sex was beginning to have a adverse mental affect on me. I felt like I was using her, but of course I knew I was only using her for sex, money wasn't a part of the deal. The longer we stay together the larger the amounts grew. Weeks later I finally got a break from her, because of my swimming ability I was selected to go to the Navy seal water survival training in san Diego on the other side of the blue Coronado Bridge. She drove me to the airport that evening, as we stood waiting for the plane she noticed two Hollywood celebrities walking pass and pointed them out to me. One was my favorite actor in the world and the other one became famous years later because of his infamous double homicide.

Before getting on the plane she shoved a wad of hundred dollar bills, totaling $500 in my pocket. I quickly took the money out of my pocket and put it back in her hand. She became quite upset and shove the money in my pocket and dramatically ran off down the ramp and out to the parking lot. Once I return from the water survival training she pick me up from the airport and drove me to a nightclub parking lot, before the car was in park she stripped down to her panties and grabbed me by the collar dragging me into the backseat. She was on fire, but I gave her the right hose to extinguish all her flames of desire.

After three hours of pulsating sex she pulled out her cigarettes and a wodd of $100.00 dollar bills from her purse, she stuff the money in my shirt pocket.

I said, "What are you doing, please! Don't give me anymore money," She looked at me and said, "keep it, it's for your birthday".

"My birthday is more than six months away" I said.

"Well just keep it anyway, just keep it for me".

I counted the money and it came to $600. Now I was really beginning to feel like a whore, I try turning the money down on several occasions and even asked that she not give it to me anymore, but she was relentless as though she didn't hear a word I said. Every time I saw her, she was pulling off her panties, diving into the backseat of the car. We were having sex so much I thought my penis was going to go into a coma.

Three months went by and we were having sex every day, three or more hours during each sexual encounter, it was beginning to be more than I could bare, the money, the sex and the gifts. It was as if she was buying me and I have no choice in the matter but to be brought. I knew I had to do a disappearing act, so I stop calling and meeting her. Two weeks went by and I hadn't heard a thing and all the sudden a Young Cpl. came into the office yelling about a crazy lady at the legal office telling one of the attorneys Cpl. Gray Robbed her. I jumped from my chair like I was shot from a cannon.

"I'm Cpl. Gray"! I exclaimed, "Robbery, who was I supposed to have Robbed?"

"Their's a lady at the legal office right now saying you Robbed her". The young Marine said.

I grabbed my cover (Hat) and lit out like a bolt of lightning down the steps and onto the catwalk. Their she was standing in front of my Captains door." I grabbed her by the arm.

"What the hell are you trying to do"?

She looked at me disappointingly, then striking me on the shoulder with her fist. "You're a shit" she said, looking at me out of the corner of her eyes.

"Come on let's go" I said.

I pulled her into her car and off we went across the air strip and down to the beach. She appeared upset but I knew exactly what she wanted, so I didn't even hesitate, or put up a fight. I parked the car in a secluded place, climbed into the back seat, then let her have away. She jumped up and down on me for several hours, crying and screaming, professing her love for me, but I didn't Love her, I never loved her, therefore; I set unaffected by her rants and raves about how much she loved me. All I could do is what I knew how to do, I plowed it in her deep, long and hard until she relented.

After 2 hours of pulsating sex we climb back into the front seat to discuss what was on her mind. She sat behind the steering wheel of her car, lit her cigarette, reclining her seat back she paused for a minute then turning to me with teary eyes.

"Marry me Whip".

Then reaching into her book bag she pulled out $15,000 dollars cash, still band together with paper bank straps, looking as though the money came straight off the press. She placed five stacks of money on my lap. I took a deep breath and thought about the possibilities of a better life. My wife has already left me once and it wouldn't surprise me if she did it again. I just looked at Luz suggestively as if I might consider taking her offer. Talking to myself.

"only if I wasn't already married, it would be possible".

My marriage was in ruins, but I had to give it another chance. I've known May since the third grade and beside she's the mother of my child, I had to see my marriage through to the end. Luz reached across the seat and grab my hand, squeezing it, nervously looking deep into my eyes, she increased her offer to giving me half of $875,000.00 dollars.

"Where are you going to get that kind of money?" $15,000 is one thing but $875,000 is another. I didn't believe her of course, so she pulled out a letter from the real estate Company located in Los Angeles. The letter stated the airport wanted to purchase her land located right outside of the fence line. The land was large enough to occupy 14 homes. It wasn't even a second thought, I knew she wasn't a young woman. She was 52 years old, she would need the money to support herself a lot sooner than I. I was only 28 years old and have a full life ahead of me, she was already at the halfway point between life and death. I didn't want to take her money. I didn't even feel comfortable with the $40 she was jamming in my pocket after every sexual encounter.

It reminded me of the time my mother would make me cut my elderly neighbors grass. They could not afford to pay me because they were on a fixed income, and my mother reminded me not to take their money. But the old man refused to let me cut his grass without giving me something, so he shove three dollars in my pocket once I finish cutting his yard. Although the old man paid me, I still learned the lesson my mother was trying to teach me. Help someone who can't pay you back. In other words, it doesn't cost anything to be kind. With this life lesson I never used a women or anyone else for that fact and I wasn't about to start with using Luz, so I turned down her offer. We parted ways that evening and I never saw her or heard from her again. I guess she finally got the message that I couldn't be bought. That was a crazy sexual maze I would never forget and all of a sudden I wasn't mad at May for being such a horrible wife anymore. I miss Luz, I often felt the absent of her presences. Most of all, our sex wasn't on a schedule and it lasted far longer than 10 minutes.

I didn't have to pretend I was anything other than my self when I was with Luz, I didn't have to give her handfuls of money, I didn't have to constantly entertain her. I didn't have to beg her to cook a decent meal or have unplanned sex, and most importantly I didn't have to explain to her how to treat her man when he's trying his best. Six months had gone by and I was still living in Hawaii alone, I hung out at the beaches and seemingly had my pic of the foreign tourists, but I decided to let it pass me by because I didn't believe I could endure another crazy romance. May refused to return home and I refused to let my marriage end but I wasn't going to kiss her butt or beg her to come back.

Finally May's mother told her she couldn't live with her, she convinced her that she was grown and married and needed to be with her husband. So she returned seven months after she had departed. She looked horrible, her face was broken out with acme from constantly eating french fries and potato chips. I could tell by her attitude she didn't want to be here but she had no choice at this point in her life. As she came out of the terminal I notice she only had my youngest daughter with her. I went to the terminal door and peek down the hallway, I turned around and hunch my shoulders.

Asking, "Where are the girls?". "I didn't bring them" she said,

"Well that's fucking obvious, why not?" I didn't have the money, She said,

"I told you to go to the military administrative office on Arlington Blvd and they would have issued you free tickets for them.

I couldn't believe she had done such an insensitive thing, I was in furious. I told her to bring my girls with her when she returned but she purposely ignored me after I requested that she bring them with her. I needed to see my girls and I wasn't leaving the island until they had a chance to experience it for themselves. I began to pull out all stops, any and everyone I could talk too that had authority, I did just that, and two weeks later I flew to Indianapolis and brought my girls to Hawaii. I believe my deceased wife was speaking to me from the grave, I felt compelled to have my girls with me and not 5000 miles across the ocean. Somehow I knew Michaela was struggling with her emotions and she needed to be around her dad.

I arrived at my mothers house two weeks later on Monday afternoon. I walked in the door, my mother was standing in the kitchen ironing my girls clothes and packing their suitcases. My daughters looked up and saw me and both came running with arms wide open. I kneeled down on one knee to huge both my girls. I squeeze them tight as if I hadn't seen them in years. Michaela smiled from ear to ear, happy as she could be to see her dad, it made me feel good that I could go get my girls and bring them back to Hawaii with me. I could feel the distance between us and I had to have them with me at all cost.

The plane was so crowded I couldn't get tickets to sit in the same roll with my daughters, but someone was kind enough to switch seats with me so that we could all sit together. The five hour flight was grueling, Miya became very fidgety after two hours in the air, so I let her walk up and down the aisle to stretch her legs, then eventually she fell asleep and didn't awake until we landed in Hawaii. This was probably one of the happiest times of my life. I was very glad that I could give my girls this experience. Once we landed I was surprised, May drove to the airport to picked us up, and for once she even seemed happy with their arrival. I could blame her for being a horrible wife, but she seemed to be a much better mother than she was a wife. I still didn't trust her fully with my children, she was in emotional wreck, but very experienced with consealing her devious plans. Confused about what she wanted to do in life and who she wanted to be. Rather than paying her own way through college, she blamed the Reagan administration for her academic short comings, not being able to finish her training in television production due to financial aid cut backs. Blaming would become her trademark in our marriage, blaming everyone for everything around her, instead of fixing her life herself. I believe she was internally depressed and wanted me to give her something that I was ill-equipped to provide, 'a sense of purpose'.

Often I would find May setting on the couch at two in the morning watching TV. I watched her from a distance as she sat quietly eating her bowl of Ramen noodle with a glass of peppermint snaps tucked beside her thigh slightly out of view.

I asked "Why are you sitting out here at 2 AM in the morning?"

She said, "You cry in your sleep over Cindy" and it drives me crazy.

I guess I never got over my wife's passing. I thought about her constantly, I couldn't help it, she was a permanent part of my memory, set deep in my murky subconscious, thoughts of her were automatic, she was forever fermented in my head. I quest May couldn't compete with the thought of another women hanging out in her house, the thought of their mothers sprit watching over her children scared May partly out of her mind.

Months passed and I thought I would have forgotten about Luz by now, but every time I sat on the beach and let the ocean water wash up against my feet, thoughts of her come home like truth. I smile everytime I thought about her and her crazy ways. The way she loved me unconditionally and the freedom I felt when I was with her.

Those are good memories, but when I left the beach and returned to my house and walked through the door all those good memories fade away into thin air, returning me to a sobering assessment of reality. I was sick of surviving on a E-4 salary and having a wife that complains about money but never attempted to earn any. I was sick of being depressed, and being in a dysfunctional marriage. I was sick of not being able to make love to my wife anytime I wanted too. I was sick of not having a good home cooked meal and most of all was just sick of being sick and tired. However; I did get some joy out of life, Sgt. ving got his comeuppance that year. A young Lance Cpl. was standing fire watch, he got bored in the middle of the night and decided to take a hit of acid.

At first the acid had very little effect on him, he lost his patiences, so he decided to take another hit. Within seconds of the second hit of acid the Young Lance Cpl. began to flip out. He called the officer of the day requesting to go to the hospital. The officer of the day asked him what did he take? the young marine refused to answer the officers question. The officer told the young marine.

"I'm not going to transport you to the hospital until you tell me what you took and who you got it from".

The Young Lance Cpl. Inform the officer that Sgt. ving sold him the drugs. The next morning Sgt. King was arrested and escorted to the Brig. After his trial he received five years in Leavenworth prison in Kansas City. I wasn't jumping for joy over another man's misery, but I couldn't help but smile when I walk pass my Captains desk. I gave him the stink eye and a smirky look, with a broken smile.

I said to myself," How do you like those green eggs and ham, asshole?"

I couldn't believe they gave that shit Bird my Sgt. Stripes, but it all worked out in the end for the better good. Before I knew it we were shipped back to 29 Palms Desert for 12 weeks, I couldn't wait to get this trip over with because it will be my last trip to Twentynine Palms and when I return to the base I will have at exactly 12 months left in the corp. Once again we reached the Twentynine Palms base and drove all night into the desert until we were far from the main base, as soon as the trucks stopped, I jumped out the back and dust a pound of sand off my uniform.

Sgt. Tubman called out my name while simultaneously tossing me a round ball. I reached up and caught the ball with my hand. The ball turned out to be a small cactus cover with thorny pin pricking Needles. I shaked my hand violently trying to get the cactus off my skin, the harder I shook my hand the more the cactus crawl up my arm. I stopped flinging my arm around long enough to take out my K bar knife and cut the cactus off my arm. I looked at Sgt. Tubman with a look that could kill, but all of a sudden I had an idea. I began walking around picking up the small cactus with a pair of wire cutters, placing them in my Cover and storing them under my cot for later that evening.

I patiently waited all night until everyone was asleep. I walked off a hundred meters from the Canon and fired up a heat tap to make a cup of mocha. I left my stove burning, making the fire watch Believe I was 100 meters away cooking. To distract the fire watch I tossed a can in the opposite direction of their position, like idiots they follow the noise, then I crept up the hill to the Captains tent. I stood outside the tent for several minutes to ensure he was asleep. I could here low tone snoring coming from inside the tent, so I put on my night vision goggles and stepped inside the tent quickly as though I was reporting in. I shine my flashlight with the red lens around the room and "bingo" there he was lying on his side with his back towards the door. It couldn't have been a more perfect situation. I creeped over step-by-step, using my wire cutters I sat each cactus from head to toe Down inside of the sleeping bag, then I crapped out of the tent and back to cooking my coffee and cocoa 'Mocha'.

    I lay on my cot and nibble on a chocolate bar from my C rations. I stare up into the emptiness of the night, watching the stars race across the sky. I love the twilight hours, it was my favorite time in the universe, the entire world was dead to me, everything was standing still. It was as if I was the only survivor after an apocalypse.

    At 4 AM I could hear my first Sargent and Captain talking in a very low voice and all of a sudden the Captain bursting out of the tent yelling and screaming as he ran out into the Baron desert, clawing and ripping at his back trying to remove the cactus that rolled all over his body as he shake vigorously trying to remove the cactus balls. Two Marines tackle him while a third tried to extract the cactus balls a with pair of pliers. I sat quietly in front of my Canon heating a cup of coffee while I watch the spectacle unfold. I didn't even pretend like I was going to help him or cared. I laughed so hard I almost spilled a very good cup of mocha. Fragging him almost made me feel better about not being promoted to Sgt. I was able to move on with my Marine Corp career that I knew would end in a few short months, I was no longer angry at the Capt. are the Marine Corps for that fact. I was done with the idea of serving my country and I no longer wanted to play Marine. My new life and the civilian road I was about to face, would challenge me, emotionally, physically, and financially to the limits of stress I have yet to encounter.

    Our time being stationed in Hawaii and my military service has come to an end. I sent my family back to Indianapolis while I looked for work and a place to live in Los Angeles California. I left the base with

$640.00 dollars to my name and a bus ticket to Los Angeles. I stayed in a rundown hotel in the center of downtown Los Angeles that had a community bathroom I shared with six other families and roaches the size of my thumb.

It was my first time staying in downtown LA and I wasn't taking any chances so I hide the remainder of my fortune behind the roach patrolled mirror in my room and ventured out onto the streets of Los Angeles. The sidewalks were smother with the dispossessed living in card board boxes and panhandling for money. I had little money but felt come pelt to share what I had with those less fortune than myself, little did I know it was faith come calling. I was riding the city bus looking for work but not making much progress, so I decided to walk around the city and take in the sights. At last I saw a big party at a small park across the street.

"This looks like fun I thought."

So I made my way toward the park. Just as I stepped off the side walk a huge city bus came to a screeching halt right in front of me, the doors fling wildly open.

"Get on the bus'. The bus driver said. I looked at him with a puzzled look. "What?"

I said. Get on the bus! Adamantly he saids this time. "I don't have anymore bus money" I said.

That's ok I will take you a few blocks. We traveled about a mile, before the bus driver explain the reason for picking me up. He said the park I was head toward is a gang members park, where the Southern Mexican gangs hangout. I thought for sure at the moment my guardian angels were truly watching over me. Later that evening I stayed close to the hotel, not walking more than two blocks in any given direction. I peeked in the windows and to my surprise I was able to watch a television soap opera being filmed.

I walked the streets and rode the bus lines for two days looking for work; everywhere I went it seemed as though they were shooting a movie. Extras for the movie were lined up on the street, the motion picture cameras were on high lifts, other personnel were carrying boom microphones. I thought it was cool to see a movie made up close and personal but I had more pressing issues to think about, my money was dwindling fast due to hotel and food expenses.

I had to make a decision due to my shortage of funds and the lack of resources, I was forced to return to my enclave in Indianapolis. The bus ride was 2 1/2 days long. Sitting in an upright position with an empty stomach made the trip extra difficult. The bus made several stops and pick people up from the middle of nowhere, alone beside the road and near corn fields. Some of the bus stations were just local bus stops with a sign sticking out of the ground attached to a metal pole in the middle of nowhere. I felt very vulnerable and insecure as I stood in total darkness, three hours waiting all alone in some desolate spot for the bus to arrive. The bus trip home cost $180.00 using up all the money I had left. I didn't even have money for food. I rode the bus for 2 1/2 days, with an uneasy feeling settling in my stomach. I was starving until one kind gentle man struck up an idle conversation about the military. I listened as he spoke, I passively shake my head in agreement while my stomach grout loudly. He stop talking long enough to reach into his sandwich bag and offered me a vegetarian lettuce and cheese sandwich, normally I wouldn't accept food from strangers, but under these circumstances I grabbed the sandwich without hesitation and gormandize the sandwich to nothing but crumbs in my hand.

I arrived in Indianapolis on Monday evening about four pm. It was a much different feeling than living in Hawaii, the Air even smelled different, it felt heavier and wet. I took my seabag out of the bottom of the bus storage and walked from the bus station to my mothers house. It was about a 3 mile walk. I couldn't help but reminisce about the time I walked home from downtown Indianapolis after spending all my money on a new pair of converses tennis shoes.

Everything seemed so different and new. A new wave of Hispanics migrated into the area making the city polychromatic as well as multicultural. It was a far cry from when I was a child, the city was primarily occupied by blacks and whites, with a very small population of Asians. I had never seen a Hispanic person until 1978 when I enter Marine Corps. The city had changed drastically, I was so amazed by the new features in the city and the Scenic view I was getting, I didn't even notice how far it was from the bus station to my mothers house. It was a strange feeling as I walked down Meridian Street. The street seemed different and very familiar, and before I knew it I was turning the corner at Saul Subway. I couldn't help but smile as I look at the empty parking lot, full of memories the younger generation will never know about. I stood on the rendezvous part of the sidewall where I met Cindy for the first time, I paused to consume the essence of her memory and allow my mind to capture the moment that change my life forever. I was uncertain about a lot of things in my life but I wasn't uncertain about Cindy's menacing presences.

www.ingramcontent.com/pod-product-compliance
Lightning Source LLC
Chambersburg PA
CBHW070945080526
44587CB00015B/2226